A TIME TO BE BORN,
A TIME TO LIVE,
A TIME TO DIE.

A LIVING LEGACY by
Michael B. Kaminski

Table of Contents

Introduction and Dedication

"Your story is the greatest legacy that you will leave to your family and friends. It is the longest-lasting legacy that you will ever leave to your heirs"

(Steve Saint, pilot, and author)

This is my story,

What will be your story?

What will be your legacy?

I hope my story about my life will live long after I leave this world.

Do you ever think about how you will be remembered when you leave this life?

As I begin to create this introduction into my story and legacy, I hope to create the beginning setting…

The place: Lewisburg, Pennsylvania

The year: 2023

The date: December 24th, Christmas Eve

The time of day: Early afternoon

I find myself walking along a trail near my apartment complex where I have been living since June of 2022 after being discharged from Northern Dauphin Nursing and

Rehabilitation Center in Millersburg, Pennsylvania. In July of 2020, I went into a coma. By a miracle of God, I returned to this life in October of 2021 and lived nine months in recovery from a coma that no one expected me to survive. While in the coma, I suffered a stroke and COVID-19 two times. Suddenly, I fell out of bed in October of 2021 and I returned to the reality of this life. Although, I really did not want to return. However, I had to learn how to walk again and live independently before I could be discharged.

As I walked along the lonely trail, I had an eerie feeling. The air was surreal as if I was in a dream. After all, I had lived in a dreamlike state of existence when I was in a coma. And now I realize or have a vision of what Eternity will be like in the future because I believe that I died in a coma. And I am actually looking forward to dying.

The sky was dark, grey, and overcast. It was Christmas Eve and no one was out and walking. Although it was dark the weather was not cold. I had a strange feeling.

I began to talk aloud to myself and think about my life. I would be 77 years old in two months. I was in the "winter" of my life. When I think about the journey, the cycle of life, the "springtime" is when we are born, a feeling of new life. The "summer" is our youth and young adult years. The "fall" is our middle age years. And our senior years are when we are old, the "winter" of our lives. As I thought about my life, I began to reflect on my life, my mortality, and the end of my life. When I thought about the end of my life, I wondered about what I had done and if I had accomplished anything worthwhile or important. Had my life been worth living?

I thought about my coma and my life before my coma. And I wondered why God put me in a coma for only a short period of time and then gave me back my life here on earth. And what really caused my coma? I had not been sick. I had not had any serious accidents.

After I had been released from the nursing and rehabilitation center, I had to make an appointment with my physician as a follow-up to my discharge. While in rehabilitation, I had a CT (CAT) Scan and it was positive. There was no damage to my brain from my coma. My mind and memory were still good. I could remember my childhood. However, my doctor said that my coma was the result of a brain hemorrhage. Two liters of fluid had been drained from my brain on the first day of my coma. What caused the brain hemorrhage?

And so, I wondered why God placed me in this condition for only a year and a half and then returned me to this life. Why did God save my life, again? I should have died many times in my life from my early years in Vietnam and Southeast Asia, my very violent years as an undercover police detective living in drug groups and organized crime, and all those accidents that I had when I was driving drunk. However, God saved me every time, even when I thought that I was not worth saving. Now, why did God bring me back to life in this life, again?

As I walked along the path, I found a bench. I decided to sit down and reflect on my life.

Why was I born?

Why did I live during this time in history, the 40s, 50s, 60s, 70s, and the 80s? They were probably the best times in history.

Why was I born to the parents who raised me? They were wonderful parents compared to some of the stories that I heard from my friends.

Why was I born and raised Roman Catholic?

Why am I Polish and Italian?

Why did I grow up in Baltimore, Maryland?

Why did some of my high school friends have to die in Vietnam while I lived?

Why did P. J. Werner come into my life?

Why did Sharon, my second wife, have to die?

How do I want to be remembered after I die?

I had to smile when I thought about why I wanted to be a police officer in the beginning. I did not like the police. However, I did like the thought of carrying a gun again. I remember my first encounter with the police when I was a young boy. It was on a Halloween night and a couple of us good little boys were just having fun in the neighborhood and someone called the police on us. As I was being chased by the police, I ran through a hedgerow of low shrubs that was, unfortunately, lined with barbed wire. Not only did I tear my jeans, I tore my right leg. Even at 77 years of age, I still carry that scar. And then, the next time I had an encounter with the police, it was a couple of months after I had been discharged from the Air Force. I had gotten drunk at a dance and while driving home, I thought I saw a car in front of me and I turned to the right and passed out. I drove through a chain fence, knocked down two trees, and drove through a used car lot hitting eight cars that were for sale. When I woke up, the engine of my car was on fire. Fortunately, this "minor" accident occurred right across from Dunkin Donuts and several police officers were drinking coffee. I was arrested for driving while intoxicated and lost my license to drive for a year. So, I did not have any good thoughts about police

After reflecting on the meaning and purpose of my life for half an hour on that cold bench, I decided to walk back to my apartment. As I walked, I thought about how empty the holidays have been since Sharon died. I had come to the point where I had almost hated Christmas. And that was not a good way for an ordained minister to think. But, then, I had to think of why I wanted to be a Protestant minister. After all, I had been raised Roman Catholic. I had only been converted to the

Protestant faith for a month before entering Lancaster Theological Seminary in Lancaster, Pennsylvania. I had never read or opened a Bible before seminary. However, now, I could not even listen to Christmas music. I had lost the spirit and chose to stay away from people during this time of the year.

When I returned to my small one-bedroom apartment, I sat down and began to look around the living room. The first thing I noticed was an old 108 SP 105 mm Howitzer mortar shell that I had picked up in Vietnam and had chromed. When I read the words that I had engraved on it, I had to smile. The inscription said "TERAZ NOC PIJE. JUTRO BEDZIE LATA". Translated from Polish, it meant "Tonight we drink. Tomorrow we fly." I thought about our pilots back in those days. Most of us were "high" on something when we were flying into and over Vietnam. But, then, we did not care about life or death.

When I looked at the old mortar shell that I had picked up in 1967, I realized that I had been an alcoholic since my senior year in high school. I graduated in 1965. However, I had not had a drink of alcohol since my birthday, February 21, 1989. I will never forget the night of my last drink. I was preparing to graduate from seminary and a couple of the professors confronted me with an "intervention". I had been drinking every day in seminary since I entered in September of 1986. On the night of my "intervention", I was given two choices. Either go to treatment that night or walk out of seminary in the morning. I decided to walk toward treatment that night and I never turned back to alcohol. To this day, I believe that God directed me into seminary and ministry to save my life because I was suicidal.

As I looked around the living room, I realized that I could sum up or define my entire life with the few possessions that I had saved in two small rooms.

Next to my old mortar shell was a university mug that had the year 1973 on it. The mug was Sharon's reminder from her years at Bucknell University. Sharon was brilliant. She had graduated from a prestigious Ivy League university with a degree in Psychology. I never really could understand why she liked me. However, Sharon died only six and one-half years after we came together.

As I examined the material "things" that I had, I smiled. They were only a small fraction of what I possessed before I went into the coma. However, when no one, not even the doctors or medical staff, expected me to recover, my home, property, and all my personal possessions were sold at a Sheriff's Sale. But then, I surprised everyone and came back to this life. Fortunately, I negotiated with the attorney representing the people who bought everything. They were my neighbors. And they agreed that I could have all my personal property. However, I was only moving into a small apartment and could not take everything.

Walking around my small apartment, I began to reflect on my childhood. When I thought about those early years, I had to smile again. I realized that I had wonderful parents who loved me. However, I knew, now, that I never really appreciated their sacrifices for my happiness.

I remember sitting in the back seat of our car when my parents would drive from Baltimore up to Trevorton, Pennsylvania to visit my mother's sisters and friends. When we would pass Harrisburg, I would look at the mountains and attempt to draw them. As fate would have destiny in my life, when I grew up, I would become a graphic arts illustrator in the Air Force and then work for the Bureau of Customs in Washington, D.C. as a graphic arts illustrator.

Living in Baltimore, I never saw mountains. As I sketched them roughly as a child, I would dream about living in Pennsylvania one day. And now, as I sat in my apartment, this is where I wanted to be as a child. I moved to Pennsylvania in 1985 after working as a private investigator for five years following my resignation from the police department.

When I looked at my baby picture on the top of the refrigerator, I began to think of the legacy that my parents had given to me. Attached to the base of the picture frame were a pair of my baby shoes. Back in those days, parents had baby shoes bronzed. The primary legacy that my parents gave to me was unconditional love. Next to my baby picture, I placed two model train engines. One was from a Lionel train. The other engine was from an American Flyer train set. I remember that every year, from the time that I could appreciate Christmas, my father would create a Christmas garden around the tree with those two train sets. I still have them. What a wonderful legacy given to me by my parents.

I became very emotional as I looked at the old photographs of me standing next to the Ford Fairlane that my father gave to me when I got my driver's license. I had failed the test the first two times. My parents were not wealthy, financially. However, they were very rich in love for me. And I never really appreciated their love and devotion. And that is their legacy to me. The material "things" came and went. But their love and devotion have endured long after their spirits have been lifted up into Heaven. My mother died in 2007 and my father passed away in 2014. But their spirits will always live within me until I see them again in the next life.

When I sat down on the couch, I looked across the room and began to remember other pieces of the legacy that my father gave to me. I had to smile when I saw the old fishing rods and reels leaning against the wall. I remember the times when my dad would take me deep sea fishing at Ocean City, Maryland. And then, there were the days when we would go fishing and catch crabs on the Severn River in Anne Arundel County near where we lived. Dad would rent a rowboat and outboard motor for only a couple of dollars. And we could catch all the crabs we wanted for free. Dad would talk about the house that he lived in when he was a little boy about my age. It was known as the "Bear House" in Trevorton. They did not have heat in the winter and there were holes in the roof.

And then, I remembered the times when my father would take me to the old Memorial Stadium in Baltimore to watch the Baltimore Orioles play professional baseball. I never really appreciated those moments in time when I was young. And I did not realize how fortunate I was to have parents like my mother and father.

I had to smile when I thought about the ride home from Memorial Stadium when we passed through a section of Baltimore City known as "THE BLOCK" on Baltimore Street. I would not appreciate living on "THE BLOCK" until I was an undercover narcotics detective many years later when I was living and working on the streets of "THE BLOCK". It was a fascinating and very educational place to be with all the prostitutes, pimps, drugs, and strip clubs.

And then, I had to smile when I thought about many years later after my wife, Sharon, died and I created my first magazine, "THE ONE MAGAZINE OF ARTS AND ENTERTAINMENT".

I was driving home one night, coming back from Harrisburg, when I passed a strip club and I decided to stop in and see if they wanted to take an ad in my magazine. Well, from that night, I became very good friends with the owners. I also became the minister and chaplain for the club. I officiated several marriages of the dancers. Not many ordained clergy would ever state that they were chaplains for a strip club. And so, maybe, that unique experience is part of my legacy.

On the wall, I began to gaze intently at the old Japanese rifle that my father had brought back from World War Two. It still had Japanese writing on the stock. And directly under that rifle was a Red Rider BB gun. I thought about the contrast. Below the BB gun was the jungle knife that I carried in Vietnam. And hanging on the Japanese rifle was my old worn biker hat that I wore when I was undercover in drug gangs. There are so many memories and so many parts of my legacy.

Directly above the old Japanese rifle were mounted the steer horns that I had bought for my father and shipped back to Maryland when I was stationed in Arizona after returning from Southeast Asia.

As I was about to walk into the bedroom, I looked at the heating unit near the window and saw two pieces of legacy from my parents that made me smile as I remembered the wonderful years of my youth.

Standing upright in the corner was my old Cornet. I began to think about all the wonderful memories of playing music for three years in the high school marching and concert band. And every week, my mother would give me money to take a taxi from our home in Brooklyn Park to Curtis Bay for music lessons. Then, I remembered the fun rides with my mother on the old electric trollies through Baltimore City. Those memories are part of my mother's legacy to me.

On the heating unit, I saw a very old pair of drumsticks that my dad gave to me when I was a very young boy. A very famous jazz drummer and band leader, Gene Krupa, had given the drumsticks to my dad, at some point, during the 1930s. I will cherish those drumsticks until the day I die. When I was a senior in high school, I bought a set of drums and helped to form a rock band. I also played the drums with my dad in bars when he played his accordion. I wanted to be in the rock band just to watch the girls dance because I was too shy to talk to girls. My only date with a girl in high school was my senior prom. And she played the tuba in the high school band. I never saw her again because three weeks after graduation, I was in the Air Force.

On the wall next to my Cornet, was a plaque that my father received when he retired from The Locke Insulator Company. Locke later became General Electric in Baltimore. Attached to the wood base of the plaque is an actual insulator. My father worked very hard in that plant from the year that I was born until he retired. He always told me to take one job and stay with it. He could never understand why I had so many different professions.

Then, I began to read the headings of the framed articles on the wall and stare at the old pictures hanging next to them. I looked at the old picture of me and P J. Paul Joseph Werner was my training partner in narcotics. He was also my blood brother. P. J. had been adopted and I never had any brothers or sisters. We made a bond and a pack never to trust anyone else, not even the police. When we cut our wrists one night in a 7-11 store, we blended our blood and bonded our lives together. The night P. J. died changed my life

I also have my old police ID card in a frame with my badge. The I.D. picture was taken shortly after I had been beaten and almost killed by members of the Pagans motorcycle gang. I had been with them for ten months and they thought that I was an informant. They wanted to kill me. On my ID, I have a black right eye. I can still remember the S.W.A.T. team going into the Pagan's clubhouse, putting ropes around their necks, and pulling them out of the building.

Also on the wall are two old newspaper articles that I had framed. The headline on one of the articles is from the Maryland Gazette, dated June/1976. It said: "A Tense Night On A Drug Bust". The second article was from the Baltimore Sun Newspaper dated November/1979. That headline reads: "Undercover Cop: A Month In The Life". I had to smile when I reflected on this story because it, eventually, caused me to resign from the police department.

In my apartment, there are two upright bookcases. The one bookcase holds copies of all the books that I have written:

LIFE AFTER RUSSIAN ROULETTE: REDEMPTION

DARK SOUL

SHARON'S LIGHT

THE MIRACLE OF ROOM 405

Basically, that bookshelf holds the story of my life. However, on the top of the bookshelf rests the picture of the love of my life. Sharon was the highlight and the only woman that I truly and honestly ever loved.

On the other side of the living room, sits the second upright bookshelf. Within it are probably the most important contents and documents regarding my legacy, my high school yearbook, and Sharon's yearbook from Bucknell University. When I look through my yearbook, I have a feeling of pride in what I have accomplished in life, especially in my formal education. Neither my mother nor my father went higher than the eighth grade in school. However, I have three formal university degrees, including a master's in Divinity. My other two undergraduate degrees are in Criminal Justice and Political Science. I do not think or believe that my parents understood or appreciated the work that I had to do to achieve my university degrees, especially my M.Div.

As a child, I was always the "only child". I never had any brothers or sisters and I never wanted any. And I confess that I was both selfish and spoiled as a child. When my cousins would come to visit with my aunts and uncles, I would hide all my toys because I did not want anyone else to play with them. Now, when I think about it, my cousins probably voted me as the least likely cousin to ever live the life that I later created. And I do not think that even my parents ever appreciated what I did in life. I never told them what I experienced or did undercover in drug groups and organized crime.

In my bedroom, hanging on the walls, if you can read between the lines, are brief outlines of the most important aspects of my legacy.

Again, I have to smile when I read the first two citations on the wall. The first document is the Mayor's Citation from the Mayor of Baltimore City that is dated April/1981. However, the second citation, awarded in connection to the Mayor's Citation, is from the Senate of Maryland for "Outstanding Performance In The Harvard National Model United Nations Simulation" in 1981. It was awarded to me as one of the students from the Political Science department of the University of Baltimore who participated in the event. We represented Russia and I was on the Russian Security Council. Ironically, the certificate was signed by Senator Jerome F. Connell. I had worked for his law firm when I was a licensed private investigator after resigning from the police department. My work with his law firm ended when Connell and his law partner were arrested and charged with income tax evasion. I had to smile when I thought about my relationship with his law firm. On several occasions in the five years I worked for him, my old F.B.I. associate had contacted me to wear a wire and record our conversations on tape. Each time I refused. And each time that I refused, I would be arrested for

Driving While Intoxicated. I was arrested five times for DWI and one time for simply walking while intoxicated and carrying a concealed weapon. On each occasion, either the charges were dismissed, or I was found not guilty, or the police officer would simply not appear in court. I have no arrest record for any of these charges because of the senator's law firm.

Next to the citations for my participation in the Harvard National Model United Nations Simulation is my Air Force Commendation Medal and certificate for Meritorious Service awarded to me for my time in Southeast Asia and Vietnam from February 25, 1967, to March 25, 1968. Along with this citation, I have my medals and pictures of our C-130 plane after it had been hit by enemy mortar fire.

Also on my bedroom wall, I have my Criminal Justice degree and my Bachelor of Arts degree in Political Science. Along with those degrees, I have my award from

Pi Sigma Alpha from the Mu Gamma Chapter of the National Political Science Honor Society.

Next to my undergraduate degrees, I have my Master of Divinity degree from Lancaster Theological Seminary and my Certificate of Ordination from The United Church of Christ.

And from the American College of Metaphysical Philosophy, I have my Doctor of Philosophy in Theocentric Business and Ethics and my Doctor of Philosophy in Comparative Religion.

Finally, is my Certificate of Graduation from the Baltimore City Police Academy on December 20, 1973. Now, under my certificate from the police academy, I have the gun that I carried undercover, my nickel-plated stainless steel, four-inch, Smith and Wesson revolver. This gun saved my life several times. I also have my .44 magnum, four-inch, Smith and Wesson, "Dirty Harry" revolver, and my .380 semi-automatic pistol.

However, next to my guns, I have a very old framed picture of me in a sailor suit taken when I was about five years old. What a contrast. I still have to smile when I think about being a "dropout" from Kindergarten when I ran home after one day because I did not want to leave my mother.

On the wall, near the headboard of my bed, I have a large crucifix that I had bought for my parents sometime in the 1980s when I came to Shamokin, Pennsylvania to serve in my first parish after ordination. On one side of the crucifix, I have a plate with Mother Mary's head that I made in Cub Scouts. On the other side of the crucifix, I have a plate with the head of Jesus Christ that I also made in Cub Scouts. I think times have changed.

Again, I have to smile when I think of these precious symbols of my youth in comparison to the violent years in Southeast Asia, and Vietnam, and my years as a police officer, living undercover in drug groups and organized crime associations. However, they are a very significant part of my legacy.

Above the headboard of my bed, mounted on the wall, I have hung a very precious part of my legacy. It is a gift that was given to me from my home church, Trinity United Church of Christ, in Dalmatia, Pennsylvania, on the night of my ordination as a minister. The picture is the image of the hands of Jesus Christ reaching out to me. Every night, when I pray before I go to sleep, I talk to God under that picture because I believe that I have been saved by the hands of Jesus Christ.

On the wall in front of my bed, I have placed two very important pieces of my history and the creators of my legacy. One picture holds the wedding photograph of my mother and father. It is very old. Without their love, direction, and unity, I would not be alive today. The other picture is an image of my favorite aunt Mimi. Her real name was Mary. However, as a baby, I could not pronounce her name. I could only say "Mimi" and "Pussycat" when I talked to her. Mimi was always like my second mother. She loved me as a mother would love her own child. I will always love my "Mimi" and I will see her again one day in Heaven with my mother and father.

Also on the wall, I have placed the picture of the only woman I have truly ever loved in this life, my second wife, Sharon. I have decided that a major part of my legacy will be to create a legacy for Sharon. I never really appreciated

Sharon for the beautiful woman that she was in my life. And I am not talking about physical beauty. Although, in my eyes, Sharon was truly beautiful, physically.

In the six and one-half years we were together, Sharon and I never had one physically sexual moment. I never saw her body without her wearing clothes. On the first night we met, Sharon told me that she would never marry me and that she would never have sex with me. However, I fell deeply in love with Sharon that night when she explained her reasons. See, Sharon had been married before we met. Apparently, her marriage was a nightmare. As I have written earlier, Sharon was brilliant. She had graduated from an Ivy League university with a degree in Psychology. However, in her marriage, Sharon was abused in several ways, physically, mentally, emotionally, psychologically, and sexually. Because of the years of her abuse, Sharon suffered from severe Anorexia. At one time, before I knew her, Sharon only weighed 55 pounds. The effects of this disease eventually took her life. And so, part of my legacy is to tell Sharon's story.

I have lost many possessions because of my coma. However, the one possession that God returned to me was the 2003 Volkswagen Beetle that I bought for Sharon brand new. When Sharon died in 2005, she had rarely driven it because she was too ill. I will always cherish that bright yellow reminder of the woman who changed my life forever.

As I conclude this Introduction and Dedication, I think about the end of my life. I wonder what my legacy will be for people after I leave this life. What will happen to all the material possessions that I have told you about in this chapter? Will my life and my history disappear? Since I have no family, it will be as if my life never existed. All the very old black and white pictures that are stored in my closet from the lives of my parents will be destroyed. I wonder what part, if any, of my life will live long after I cease to exist? I wonder if you, the reader, ever have those thoughts?

And so, to answer those questions that I believe most of us have and think about as we come to the end of our mortal lives, I have written this book.

I have titled this contribution:

"A TIME TO BE BORN,

A TIME TO LIVE,

A TIME TO DIE"

(A Living Legacy)

This book will be presented, primarily, from a Theological perspective. It will be based on the third chapter of Ecclesiastes, verses 1-8, found in The Holy Christian Bible.

"Everything has its time.
To everything, there is a season.
A time for every purpose under Heaven.

A time to be born.
A time to die.
A time to kill.
A time to heal.
A time to break down.
A time to build up."

It will also be based on two songs from the past:

"Seasons In The Sun" by Terry Jacks (1974) and

"Turn! Turn! Turn!" by The Byrds (1965)

"The choices that we make about the lives that we live determine the kinds of legacies that we leave". (Travis Smiley)

About The Author

During a book signing session following a speaking event on "FIRST IMPRESSIONS - FALSE PERCEPTIONS", a woman approached Michael Kaminski and introduced herself. Smiling, the woman informed Kaminski that, after listening intently to his life story, she thought his journey was like identifying with a "Renaissance Man".

After thanking the woman for what he had considered to be a compliment, Mike Kaminski took a moment to reflect on the unexpected insight of the woman as she walked out of sight. See, before that night, Mike Kaminski acknowledged that he had been called many things in his life, many very descriptive titles, and some were not always very flattering; however, he could not recall ever being considered a "Renaissance Man".

See, by definition, a "Renaissance Man" (or woman) is considered to be well-educated, talented, knowledgeable, and very proficient in many fields of expertise.

Now, as Kaminski continued to reflect on the comment made by the unknown woman, he began to analyze his life later that evening. And, upon reflection, Mike Kaminski also considered the basic meaning of "Renaissance" as it now pertained to his life after he researched the definition. See, the word "RENAISSANCE" literally is defined as meaning "REBIRTH" in French.

And so, now, Kaminski could relate to the perceptive evaluation of the very intriguing woman who had come into his life for only a brief moment in time but appeared to correctly analyze his life history. See, Mike Kaminski's journey in life had always been centered on the "Rebirth" of his life through various recreations and new identities that were dependent on the situation that he was living in and through at that time. However, Michael also had to acknowledge that, with most of his creative occupations and professional adventures, he had always been very proficient in convincing people that he was someone or something that he was not in reality in order to be accepted. See, along the way, Michael B. Kaminski had learned the art of mastering deception. Although he had earned three formal university degrees along the way in life, maybe the most beneficial education he received from living life on the streets was his informal master's degree, a Master of Deception (his M.D.).

As Mike Kaminski continued to reflect on the journey of his life in the silent darkness of his lonely motel room that night, he had to smile and admit privately that most of his adventures, truthfully, had been a series of "First Impressions - False Perceptions".

And so, Kaminski began to think about all the professions and occupational adventures that he had either talked his way into or worked his way into, with little or no experience. And then he had to smile when the 2003 movie, "Catch Me If You Can" came into his mind.

See, another definition of "Renaissance Man" in today's world is that of "a very clever person. Someone quick to understand, learn, devise, and apply ideas." Now, Mike Kaminski realized that, very early in life, he could be a very convincing "con artist".

Mike Kaminski had to smile as he thought about his life while sitting in that dark motel room, where instead of considering himself to be "cultured", as in the definition of a true "Renaissance Man", he was just simply "clever". See, for Mike Kaminski, it was always about the challenge, the game, the adventure, and the deception.

Now, Kaminski finally understood that his clever creativity in playing the "game" and his natural ability to honestly deceive people had been his greatest assets in surviving undercover in drug groups and organized crime associations for so many years. And so, maybe his creativity would now become his legacy.

Since that first night, following the brief encounter with the unknown woman, Michael Kaminski has been called a "Renaissance Man" many times in his walk through life. His formal education includes university degrees in Criminal Justice and Political Science. He also has a master's degree in Theology. However, Kaminski still confesses that his most valuable education was acquired informally through living on the streets, undercover in drug groups and organized crime, and his creative ability to talk his way into occupations and professional opportunities that he had no prior, or very little, education or experience.

After returning home from Southeast Asia, Taiwan, and Vietnam and being honorably discharged from the Air Force, Michael Kaminski found himself working for Westinghouse Corporation as a printed circuit draftsman. However, Kaminski had no prior knowledge or experience in electronics, printed circuit design, drafting, or electrical engineering. However, during the initial interview, Kaminski convinced the interview team that he had worked in the field of printed circuit design, although he did not know what a printed circuit board was and had never seen one.

Then, Kaminski worked his way into becoming the only graphic arts illustrator with the Bureau of Customs in Washington, D.C. In the interview, he convinced the team of his extensive fictitious artistic creativity by using a stolen portfolio of artwork and illustrations he had "obtained" from his supervisor before his discharge from the Air Force

Before becoming a police officer, Kaminski worked as an insurance agent for Prudential Insurance Company. He had convinced his future employer of his extensive sales history that never existed.

Following his years undercover in drug groups and organized crime associations, Kaminski created a private investigative detective agency and worked, primarily, for the criminal defense lawyers that he had worked against when he was undercover.

Eventually, Mike Kaminski relocated to Pennsylvania and creatively convinced a seminary of his religious perspective and was accepted with no theological background. In fact, he had never opened or read a Bible in his life and he was not religious. Kaminski still remembers and smiles when he was asked by his New Testament professor to present the Bible verse or scripture that he liked the best. In response, Mike Kaminski stated that he did not have a passage of scripture that he did not like because he had never opened a Bible. The professor did not like Kaminski from that day. However, Mike Kaminski did graduate from seminary, received ordination, and served in parish ministry.

Then, Mike Kaminski went to work for a county government agency as a drug and alcohol treatment specialist until he decided to create a private counseling agency with no license, no formal education, training, or experience.

Finally, before beginning to write books and present workshops, Mike Kaminski created and published two magazines with no advertising experience or training. He began his work as an author by writing five books on the founding Gurus of the Sikh Faith. However, Kaminski was not Sikh and did not know anything of the faith before he began his work.

Now, as a successfully published author, following the original books on the Sikh Faith, Kaminski has written five additional books. And he uses his creative background in his speaking topics, workshops, and seminars on "First Impressions - False Perceptions", "Mirrors and Masks", "Self-Image", and "Perception of Self".

For more information on how to contact Michael B. Kaminski, about speaking events, his books, or workshops, please contact him through his email address, mbkaminski9@gmail.com.

WHY DO WE EXIST?

"The purpose of life is not to be happy. It is to be useful, to be honorable, to be compassionate, to have made some difference that you have lived and lived well."

(Ralph Waldo Emerson, author)

I wonder, at times, lately, what part of my life, if any, will live on, long after I die?

After we physically die of this mortal life, will it be as if we never really existed?

Will the memory of our lives disappear forever?

When my life will cease to exist?

Have you ever asked yourself those questions or similar questions?

After I recovered from my coma well enough to live independently again, I moved into my future home, an apartment. As I began to unpack the contents of all the possessions that my friends had moved from my old home, I began to reflect on my new life. I had to smile as I began to examine what I now had to begin a new life.

I had given my friends several pages of items that I wanted to be returned. However, they only chose a fraction of what I had listed. After all, I was moving from a three-bedroom home with a large garage, that I had just built before my coma, into a one-bedroom apartment. I could not have everything that I asked for in the transition. However, that is what life is all about. Many times, we just cannot receive everything we hope to have and we need to appreciate the gifts that we have been given in life.

In a way, I felt like a little boy, again. I looked in the mirror and saw the image of a newborn baby. I felt as if I had been born again when I was returned to this life. See, because of my stroke, I had to learn how to walk again, just like a newborn baby taking his first steps.

In the process of unpacking what had been returned to me, I found two publications that I had saved many years earlier and had forgotten that I had them. I wondered why my friends had decided to pack these publications and leave so many of my other more expensive research books that I listed.

The publications were two issues of our old high school literary magazine, "REFLECTIONS", from 1964 and 1965 (the year I graduated). Brooklyn Park High School had been closed for many years. However, it still lives on in our memories because many of us have copies of this magazine.

I began to look through the publication and read some of the poems, short stories, essays, and reviews that had been submitted by my classmates and I had to smile, again. After all, some of us were really very creative writers, even at a young age. Unfortunately, I was not among them. And then, I found the poem that I had submitted. I thought to myself, "Did I really write that poem? It was not very good."

As I continued to look through the issue of "REFLECTIONS" from the class of 1965, my class, I found a book review that was submitted by David Johnson, one of my classmates. I had not seen or talked to David since the night we graduated. We had known each other in school all those years; however, we were never close friends. After all, David was very intelligent. He was in the Academic group. That meant he was going to college. I stayed in the Commercial group of students. Although I was not stupid, I had no desire to continue my formal education in college after graduation. Actually, I had already signed up for the Air Force because, although I wanted to go to Vietnam because of the war, I did not want to be drafted into the army.

David Johnson had submitted a book review of a novel by Thomas Wolfe titled "OF TIME AND RIVER". David titled his review "WHY DO WE EXIST?" Now, that topic fascinated me because of my new life after being "reborn" by God from my coma. As I read David's contribution, I began to reflect on my life and the meaning and purpose of my existence. Why am I still alive? Why do I exist?

And so, here is David Johnson's review. Think about it.

"Thomas Wolfe's novel, "OF TIME AND THE RIVER", left a deep impression on me. In it, the author projected his personality and thinking through his main character, Elmer

Gant, who was involved in a mad search for the meaning of time and man's relationship to it. Now, I find questions haunting me. Why do we exist? Why am I here? Are we only a whim of God? No doubt many others have entertained these same questions at some time or another.

Those who believe in existentialism feel that man is merely a whim and has no real purpose in living. They believe that while we are here, we just bide time until we die and that is the end. We no longer have existence in any form. I can well believe this kind of person may lose his mind because he truly has nothing for which to live.

As Christians, we do have a purpose in life. And that purpose is to recreate and replenish the earth; to leave a definite contribution to mankind, whether it be a work of art, a child, or only a thought.

If our lives are to be successful, we must serve mankind in some way. We dare not merely exist. If God had meant us to do only that, He would not have made us capable of doing so many things. But since God has very generously endowed us with versatile potentials, it is our duty to realize and make use of them so that, upon leaving this earth, something good will be present which was not here when we came."

After I read the book review from my old high school classmate, I just had to reflect on his insightful and very perceptive words, especially at such a young age. Now, I could see and understand why David Johnson was on the

Academic path in high school and I had chosen to go into the Commercial lane. In comparison, here is the poem that I submitted to the magazine in my senior year of high school. Now, I am amazed that it was actually accepted in "REFECTIONS". I wrote:

"I am Youth!

I am impulsive.

I act without thinking.

I live from week-end to week-end.

I exist from one summer to another.

I love music, speed, and the opposite sex.

I dread exams.

I am Youth!"

Can you see the difference in the work from my friend, David, and my submission to the literary arts magazine? When I was graduating from high school in 1965, who would have ever imagined that I would, eventually, create and publish two magazines and, then, become a successful published author? Along with the books I have written and published, I have also written five books on the founding gurus of the Sikh faith for a university professor who had been nominated for the Nobel Peace Prize.

I could not have imagined what I accomplished in my life since high school. However, I believe the perceptive insight of my classmate was, in some way, my guiding light through the darkness of many uncertain years of my existence.

Now, returning to the report by David Johnson, as it pertains to my book; first, I needed to research the definition of "existentialism". See, my philosophy in life is that if you are not certain of a topic, do not present your opinion.

"Existentialism" is defined as "a philosophical theory or approach which emphasizes the existence of the individual person as a free and responsible agent determining their development through acts of will." Now, I know that is a very technical and, maybe, confusing definition of why we exist. However, reading into it, I can see that each one of us is responsible for our own lives, that each one of us has free will, and that each one of us has the God-given potential to set goals in our lives and the power to achieve those goals if we can work toward the accomplishment and the creation of our dreams. That definition is the underlying goal for the creation of this book, using my personal life as an example.

And so, again, I ask the questions that my high school classmate presented in his essay and book review. It appears that David Johnson was advanced in his years and, maybe, an old soul at the youthful age of eighteen. I wonder, have you ever asked yourself the same questions: "Why do we exist?",

"Why do I exist?", "Why am I alive"?", "Am I only a whim of God?", "Why was I Born?"

I remember asking myself similar questions when I was sitting on that lonely bench on that dark and overcast Christmas Eve before I began to write this reflective journal of my life.

Personally, I do not believe that any of us is a "whim of God". Each one of us is a unique creation that enters into this world with so much potential from our Creator, God. Unfortunately, some of us are not wanted by our parents, some of us are abused, and many of us are thrown away like discarded trash. However, we are all creations of God and we have been blessed with a special gift, the gift of life. What we choose to do with our unique gift, for most of us, depends on our personal choices. I confess that I have wasted a high percentage of my life. And I realize that I cannot replace that lost time or start over.

My mother and father may have lived their lives with the belief that they never really accomplished anything. Both my parents were born into very poor families. As I have stated before, neither my mother nor my father went higher than the eighth grade in school. My mother pressed shirts in a factory and my father worked on the assembly line of an insulator company all his life. They both worked very long and hard to give me a good life. I never wanted or needed anything. And in their unselfish and loving way, my parents did create a legacy that would live long after they were lifted up into Heaven. The legacy that they created was in their only son. See, they gave me life. And in my life and what I have accomplished, my mother and father still live and exist.

I do believe that there is life after our mortal death in this world. For me, it is Eternity. And I believe that I have experienced a brief glimpse of Eternity when God placed me in a coma. See, that is why I am looking forward to living in Eternity. When I was existing in that state of Eternal Life, I was happy and at peace. I was with my mother, my father, and my favorite aunt Mary. And I was with my wife, Sharon. I really did not want to return to this life. However, I now understand that my coma was only a temporary state of existence. And then, God returned me to this life because there are still some goals remaining for me to achieve that are important to my final legacy.

See, before I entered into a coma, I also had doubts about my life. There were times when I asked myself all the questions that I have presented to you, the reader, to consider. However, now that I have experienced a brief glimpse of Eternity, I truly do appreciate each day that I am alive and thank God for every new day that I am granted another moment of existence in this life. Now, I truly do believe that each day that I exist in this life is a gift from God, that my life is worth living, and that my life has always had meaning and a purpose, even during the dark, grey, and overcast periods of my life.

As I take time to reflect on the past journey of my life, my existence, before my coma, I know that I have accomplished, achieved, and experienced many moments in time. However, now, I also know that I still have a contribution to give to this world and the contribution that I will give will not only be part of my legacy and reason for my existence in this life but, whatever I now contribute will also be the legacy of my parents and the reason why they existed.

Now, think about our opening quote for this section:

"The purpose of life is not to be happy. It is to be useful, to be honorable, to be compassionate, to have made some difference that you have lived and lived well."

(Ralph Waldo Emerson, author)

How have you lived most of your life?

How has the journey of your life been for you?

As I reflect on that quote from Ralph Waldo Emerson, I admit that I have traveled many roads in life. And some of those roads have not always been good or safe. Some roads have been very rough.

See, in a very unique and personal way, those roads that I chose to travel can be defined in the poem by Robert Frost from 1920, "The Road Not Taken", as roads "less traveled". Meaning, if I had not taken those rough roads, I would never have lived the life that I have experienced. If I had never traveled the roads I chose to walk, if I had made different choices in life, then, I probably would not be writing this book for you and for my legacy. However, those roads are now my story. They are significant parts of my legacy that I will leave to my friends because I do not have any family. In fact, at this stage of the journey, my friends are my "family".

I can honestly state that, for most of my journey, I have had a good life, a very interesting life, a life that I could have never imagined as a little child in my first life. I believe that I have had a successful life, even with disappointments, and I believe that I have made a difference in the lives of many people. And, yes, I have made many mistakes. I have done things that I, now, regret. I have lost at love. And I have wasted time that I can not recover. But, I am thankful to confess that I have not just "existed" in this gift we all call "life".

After returning to this life from a coma, I thank God every morning and every night before I attempt to go to sleep that God put me in a coma because it has changed my life. Now, I appreciate every new day that I live and exist in this life. I thank God every night for the family that I was born into and for all my accomplishments, achievements, and experiences, both good and those that have not been so good. See, now, I realize that I have learned from my mistakes and the roads that I have taken.

I believe that each human being, every baby that is born into this life, comes into this world with the God-given potential to be all that he or she desires to become if they are given the opportunity to be successful.

Now, before I begin to close this section, let us think about the opening quote from my INTRODUCTION AND DEDICATION.

"Your story is the greatest legacy that you will leave to your friends. It is the longest-lasting legacy that you will leave to your heirs." (Steve Saint, pilot and author).

Remember, as you journey through this book with me, that your personal story will always be, good or bad, for better or for worse, the greatest legacy that you will ever leave your family and friends. Your story will be unique and long-lasting. Hopefully, the memory of your journey will live long after your mortal life comes to an end in this lifetime. And so, what you do with your life should have an unforgettable impact on the lives you leave behind. Do not waste too much of your life. Do not just exist.

I know that the beginning of this journey you and I are taking together in this book appears to be the end of the story. However, this section is only the beginning of the story for you. In the end, remember the essay by my friend, David Johnson, "those who believe in existentialism feel that they are merely a whim and have no real purpose in living." See, just as David Johnson left his legacy for me to discover in our high school publication from 1965, you can leave your legacy in what you create in the future. Now, it is time for "REFLECTIONS".

Chapter 1: "REFLECTIONS"

"What greater thing is there for human souls than to feel that they are joined for life - to be with each other in silent unspeakable memories."

(George Elliot, author)

Before we begin this chapter, please allow me to reflect on our opening quote by George Elliot. Reflecting on the journey of my life, I do confess that I have been involved in some experiences that I choose never to speak about for the remainder of my life. I have done things that I am not proud of doing. I wonder if you, the reader, also feel the same way.

However, I can also confess that I have had moments and times in my life that are very personal and when I reflect on those chapters in my life, I feel very blessed and thankful to God. Upon reflection, I believe that I was granted two of the most wonderful parents that any child could have hoped to have in this life. And I was blessed with the love of an aunt who always considered me as her child. And I still have to smile when I was told that she, at one time in her life, was involved in a relationship with a Roman Catholic Priest. Maybe that is why my aunt never went to church.

However, as I reflect on the "chapters" of my life, I realize that Sharon came into my life only a couple of months after my aunt died. I will always believe that my aunt "Mimi" directed me to meet Sharon only after she had passed away.

See, I believe that "Mimi" did not want me to be lonely. And so, she allowed me to find Sharon because Sharon needed to live. And Sharon taught me the true meaning of real love. I know that I will never love another woman in this life because Sharon is my eternal wife, the true love of my life. Sharon died in 2005.

Now, when I reflect on our opening quote, I can relate to the words of George Elliot when he writes "What greater thing is there for human souls than to feel that they are joined for life". See, every morning and every night, I still talk to my mother, father, "Mimi", and Sharon. When I am outside, I look up to Heaven and imagine that I am speaking to their souls. In my heart and in my mind, they live within me and I know that I will be with them very soon in Eternity. See, I believe that was the reason God put me in a temporary coma - to experience Eternity.

Now, as I reflect on why I chose to title this chapter "REFLECTIONS", I see the covers of the old high school magazine that I referred to in the previous chapter. As I stated, when my friends were packing my personal items to move me into my new home, they packed two copies of an old Brooklyn Park High School (Anne Arundel County, Maryland) literary arts magazine that was published annually by the students titled "REFLECTIONS". I still cannot understand why my friends selected those two old publications and did not pack many of my expensive research books and Bibles.

However, the cover of the 1964 issue, which was only Volume 9, of "REFLECTIONS" had an image of a very pretty girl. I can still remember her because I always thought that she was beautiful. But she was a senior and I was only a junior. And I never had the courage to talk to her because I did not believe that she would ever be interested in me. I wonder where she is now?

The cover was interesting because the image was split. It was as if she was looking in a mirror and her reflection was a distorted, unattractive illusion. I have looked at that cover several times since beginning to write this book. I have, also, looked in the mirror many times and seen an ugly distorted reflection of the person that I was in my life and who I am today. I wonder what or who you see reflecting at you when you look in the mirror?

And now, as I look through the pages of the two old publications and read the names of all the young students who contributed poems, essays, and short stories, I have to smile because I know many of those young souls have died since 1964 and 1965. The magazine has died. And, although the building still remains, the high school has died. However, in my mind and memory, they all still live and exist because two people saved two magazines for me to cherish.

So, how would you define a "Reflection"? I always only thought of a reflection coming from an image in a mirror, or from the sun glistening, or shining, or reflecting off a river or larger body of water. Or, maybe, our shadow, on a very bright and sunny day.

Upon research, I discovered several definitions of "Reflection" that I never thought about, however; I need to consider them in the writing of this book. Now, think about these definitions:

- A thought, idea, or opinion that is formed as a remark.

- A result of meditation.

- A transformation.

- A consideration of some subject matter, idea, or purpose.

- Serious thought or consideration.

I believe that each one of those definitions can be applied to the contents of this contribution in the following chapters. See, I believe that this book is a reflection, the reflecting account of my life. The aspects that I have described previously are reflections of my life. And I am a reflection of my parents.

And, ironically, my apartment in Lewisburg, Pennsylvania, is direct across the street from a shop that Sharon's father and uncle established many years ago. Sharon and I would stop in, periodically, to visit with her relatives. Now, on a very bright and sunny day, the sign on the wall, Fisher's Meat Market, will reflect very brightly into my apartment window and I will smile and reflect on my years with Sharon.

See, each one of us is a reflection of our past, our family of origin, our family history, how we have lived our lives, what we experienced in life, what happened to us, our choices in life, and our decisions.

As I reflect on my childhood, I remember walking with my mother and Aunt "Mimi" from our home to "Doc" Harrison's Tavern on clear nights. My father was a bartender, part-time, there when he worked at Locke Insulator Company. As we walked, my mother would tell me to look up at the clear sky and see all the bright shining stars in the darkness of the night. My mother would tell me that each star is a reflection of someone's soul looking down on us as we walked. I never forgot those words from my mother. That is part of her legacy to me.

And now, when I walk, there are times when I stop and look up at the sky, up to Heaven, and I know in my heart what I believe in my mind. See, I know that my mother, my father, my Aunt "Mimi", and my wife, Sharon are all looking down at me and smiling. I know that they are watching over me, protecting me, and waiting for me.

One very interesting definition of "Reflection" that I can honestly relate to; however, I never really associated with the topic until lately, is "A result of meditation". Now I believe that, by the Grace of God, my mind and my memory were saved after I returned to this life from my coma to share my story.

I can still reflect and remember the beautiful quiet hours walking along the Susquehanna River near my home in Dalmatia before my coma and watching the flow of the water run south toward Harrisburg. And then, trying to visualize the water flowing south toward Baltimore, Maryland, my city of birth and new life.

And then, I would stop walking and sit on an old tree branch that had been broken and I would stare at the ripples in the water and meditate on my life. I would reflect on how fortunate I was to still be alive and think about all the times when I should have died. And then, I would reflect on my mother, father, Aunt "Mimi", and the love of my life, Sharon.

As I would sit on that dead old tree branch, I would throw stones into the river and watch the ripples flow south. I would think about the years and the chapters of my life as "ripples" in the "River of Life".

See, "The River of Life", is defined, as "symbolizing the passage of time (or time passages"). It is the cyclical nature of our existence and the interconnectedness of all living beings."

Briefly defined, "The River of Life" embodies the ebb and flow of all of our life experiences. It serves as a reminder of the impermanence and ever-changing nature of our journey in life.

Then, I would walk home and read about The River of Life in my Christian Bible and reflect on the almost final words found in the Book of Revelation, Chapter 22:1, which is almost at the end of the Bible, "And then He showed me a pure river of water of life, clear as crystal, proceeding from the throne of God and of the Lamb." (The New King James Version of the Holy Bible).

It was not long after I would reflect, almost daily, on the water flowing in the Susquehanna River, that I would go into a coma in July of 2020. And then, God would give me a glimpse of my future home in Eternity.

Now, after recovering from my coma, I still take long walks and reflect on the journey of my life, even on the cold days of winter, because I am so very thankful for each new morning and see the dawning of a new day.

As I continue to write this book, I have to smile because I am in the "Winter" of my life. However, I know and believe that I am getting closer to the "dawn" of a new life, the beginning of a new life, the "Springtime" of a new life in Eternity.

And just like the dark days of winter, the days of my life are getting shorter. I cannot walk as fast as I could when I was in the Springtime and Summer of my mortal life. However, I do walk as much as possible because physical exercise is good for my Parkinson's Disease just like daily meditation and praying are good forms of exercise for my spiritual health and well-being.

And now, as I begin to leave a legacy, I believe that each one of us goes through the Seasons of our lives each day of our lives. Think about it. When we wake up in the morning, it is the "springtime" of a new day, a new birth, when we open our eyes and come alive, again. Then, we go through the morning hours that become our "summertime". Eventually, the sun begins to set and go down and we go into the "fall" of our day. And, finally, toward the end of our day, we experience the "winter" before we go to sleep as if we die of this life.

Chapter 2:
"LEAVING A LEGACY"

"What is a legacy? It is planting seeds in a garden that you will never see."

(Lin-Manuel Miranda, playwright)

For me, writing a book is not easy. And beginning a new chapter requires taking time, thought, and preparation. I really had to think about how to begin this chapter of my life and legacy. Then, I found the opening quote that you just read. And so, for a moment, let us consider the thoughts and words of Lin-Manuel Miranda. "What is a legacy?"

Among many other accomplishments, Lin-Manuel Miranda created the Broadway musicals, "In The Heights" and "Hamilton". And so, I believe that he has created a legacy that will last past his lifetime. In his quote for us, Miranda states that a legacy is "planting seeds in a garden that you will never see". Now, upon reflection, I agree with this definition.

See, as I reflect on the journey of my life, I, now, realize that I have been "planting seeds" for people to think about a long time after I am gone from this life.

And, as I reflect on my legacy and what I will leave for others when I die, I know that it will not include money. However, I believe that my legacy will be more valuable to many people if they understand the value of my legacy. As I

9

reflected on my life, I believe the one gift that I can leave people is to live with "Resilience". To develop a sense of toughness and to recover from difficulties that will either be created or unexpectedly occur in your life.

Think about my life. As a young boy, I could never have imagined becoming a graphic art illustrator. I had no artistic talent. And, when I was preparing to graduate from Air Force basic training, after being set back because I could not run the obstacle course, I was assigned a career field as a Draughtsman. I did not know drafting in high school. And so, when I reported to my first assignment in Washington, D. C., I was informed that the general had requested an Illustrator. So, my career field was immediately changed to Illustrator. And, again, I did not know how to illustrate or draw. However, I learned very quickly. And that knowledge, eventually, led me to a position with the Bureau of Customs in Washington, D. C. as a graphic arts illustrator.

And then, when I became a police officer, I was transferred to undercover narcotics. If any of my friends from high school had told me that I would ride a motorcycle and be involved with the Pagans motorcycle gang, I would have never believed them.

However, as I continue leaving a legacy of "resilience" and keeping focused on what you want to achieve and accomplish in life, I offer my journey into ordained ministry.

After five years of working as a licensed private investigator, primarily, for the criminal defense lawyers that I worked against in narcotics, I began to think about my life and I wondered why I was still alive. I had been Roman Catholic my entire life. After many years of living undercover in drug groups and organized crime associations, taking lives, and having three contracts to kill me taken out on my life, with two contracts almost successful, and then working as an investigator for criminal defense lawyers, I wanted to drop out of society. Plus, I had been an alcoholic since I was a senior in high school. Since I was Roman Catholic, I decided to become a Priest. And so, I made an appointment to talk to my Bishop about my desire to enter a Catholic Seminary. Bishop Murphy had been a priest at my parish since I was a little boy. He gave me my first Holy Communion. I truly respected him as a priest.

When I confessed my intentions and desires to become a priest, Bishop Murphy, in a very serious manner, confronted me and denied my request. He refused to grant me an endorsement. His reasons were very clear. He told me that I was an alcoholic and that I enjoyed intimate relationships with women.

Although his rejection and disapproval were honest, I agreed with Bishop Murphy's decision. Shortly after that confrontation, I moved to Pennsylvania to get away from everyone and my past relationships. All I did for six months was drink and try to forget about my past. I became very suicidal. And then, God changed my life in a way that I never expected to happen.

On a fateful day in March of 1986, while I was driving drunk, I went to sleep at the wheel and drove my car into a house directly across from the only church in Dalmatia, Pennsylvania, where I had been living, Trinity United Church of Christ.

I hit the front of the house with such an impact that I moved the front porch away from the building. I almost died in that accident. At the medical center, I was placed on morphine. The minister from Trinity United Church of Christ came to visit me on several occasions. During one visit, I informed Reverend Miller that I wanted to become a priest because I was Roman Catholic. Reverend Miller was aware of my social life because I had been attending his Sunday worship church services. After consideration, Reverend Miller suggested that I consider entering the Protestant ministry because I could get married again if I found someone to love. After reflection and serious thought, I agreed. I could still perform all the duties of a Roman Catholic Priest.

During my weeks in the medical center, recovering from my near-fatal accident, while on morphine, I would experience hallucinations and take "trips". Every day, I would take a "trip" to somewhere in New England at a period during the 1700s. On each "trip", I would meet a woman that I could never touch. However, I grew deeply in love with her. I never knew her name.

In September of 1986, when I could walk again, I entered Lancaster Theological Seminary in Lancaster, Pennsylvania. To this day, I believe that God directed me to seminary for several reasons. God saved my life because I agreed to go into alcohol recovery treatment or I would have been ordered to leave seminary and not graduate. I have not had a drink of alcohol since my birthday, February 21, 1989. However, eventually, I did graduate and receive ordination and serve in parish ministry.

I will never forget why I was finally granted ordination after being rejected in three interviews. Finally, I was asked why I wanted to be ordained. The committee suggested that I should just be a counselor. As I thought about my response, I reflected on my original hope to become a priest. However, I really did not know or have an honest reason why I desired priesthood. After I thought about my response, I told the ordination committee that I wanted to give other people the same feeling that I had been given when I made my First Holy Communion as a little boy in my Catholic church. The feeling was knowing that Jesus Christ now lived within me. The committee approved my request and granted my ordination.

I was finally ordained on November 5, 1989, at my home church, Trinity United Church of Christ in Dalmatia. It was located directly across the road from the house that I drove into more than three years earlier. However, I would not, truly, understand God's plan in my life for not directing me into the Roman Catholic priesthood until many years later.

Now, maybe you are superstitious and believe that the number thirteen is unlucky. However, I will always be thankful to God for Friday the 13th.

See, it was on Friday, December 13, 1998, when God would bring Sharon into my life, again, in this life several months after my favorite Aunt "Mimi" had passed away. I found Sharon's contact information in the local newspaper's "Personals" section (before online dating was popular). Sharon had listed her name as "Lou Bassett". Now, that name sounded strange to me. However, I liked her description and replied. Sharon responded within a couple of days and we had a long conversation. And so, after weeks of telephone conversations, we both felt comfortable enough to physically meet.

It was on that fateful Friday night, very cold, and almost Christmas Eve, that God blessed me with the love of my life. When I saw Sharon in the light of the restaurant for the first time, I knew that I had seen her before.

See, Sharon was the woman that I had known in my morphine "trips" when I was recovering from my near-fatal accident. Sharon was the woman that I could never touch in my dreams.

Now, as I reflect on my legacy, I think of the legacy that my Aunt "Mimi" gave to me. I believe that "Mimi" did not want me to be lonely. And so, she directed Sharon to me. And it is ironic that, even in this life, I could not touch Sharon, physically. See, for the entire time that Sharon and I lived together, there was never a physically sexual moment that we shared. I never made love, physically, with Sharon. In the six and one-half years that we were together, I never saw her body naked. And I am grateful to confess that I never cheated on Sharon. I respected her too much to cheat on her. I will never forget Friday, December 13, 1998.

However, now I truly understand why God did not allow me to become a Roman Catholic priest. See, if I had gone into the priesthood, I would never have met Sharon. And Sharon was my destiny. And, by the Grace of God, I did serve as a priest and share the life of Jesus Christ as an ordained Protestant minister.

If there are three very important gifts that I can leave my friends in my legacy, they are: always believing in the Power of God, always believing in yourself and your God-Given ability, and always being resilient in your life. And you can use my life as an example for those three points.

After unexpectedly returning to this life from dying and existing in a coma, I surprised everyone by waking up. No one, not even the doctors, expected me to live. However, God had other plans for me in this life. And then, as I began to recover, I was told that I would never walk again because I suffered a stroke while in the coma. Well, by the Grace of God, my resilience, my inner resistance to listen to the opinions of other people, and the power of prayer, I am walking again.

In my recovery, I was also advised that if I did venture into the world again, I could not live independently. Well, again, I proved people who doubted my resilience and I have been living in an apartment for almost two years at the time of this writing. And, finally, I was told that if I wanted to drive a vehicle, again, I would need to get approval from a doctor. Well, I had to laugh at that suggestion. I had my driver's license renewed and I am driving. I know God has plans for me and I have a strong faith in myself and belief in communication through the power of prayer with God. See, I believe that the best gift that I can leave to others in my legacy is my own example about life and living.

"FIVE FEET FROM FATE". That was the title I had planned to title a book about my fall. My father had died in 2014. I had inherited his home, an old trailer that my parents had purchased, new, in 1982 when they moved back to Pennsylvania from Maryland. The mobile home was in poor condition for several years. I had lived with my father for the last five years of his life and I will always be very thankful to God for that time. And so, I was also thankful for his home because I believed it was part of my legacy from my parents and their spirits still lived in that home.

Approximately a year after my father passed from this life, I decided to repair part of the roof because it was leaking. However, I had always been afraid of heights, although I joined the Air Force directly after high school. But then, I was young and dumb back then.

And so, I climbed the ladder and got up on the roof. I thought about what my Veterans Administration doctor had told me several years earlier. He informed me that I had severe Osteoporosis because my bones were very weak from many years of excessive alcohol abuse and that I would probably fracture or break a bone if I fell.

Well, after repairing the roof, I began the downward climb on the ladder. And I was only five rungs from the ground when it happened. I missed one of the rungs and fell to the ground. When I hit the dirt, I heard something snap and break within my body and I felt a sharp pain on my right side. And so, I just laid on the ground for a while and looked up to the sky, and prayed to God.

Eventually, I picked myself up and, even, put away the ladder. However, the pain became more intense. For six weeks, I walked with the pain in my right hip. My friends pleaded with me to go to the hospital. However, I was stubborn and refused to accept the reality that there was something damaged within me. Plus, I did not want to leave my six cats home alone if I had to go to the hospital. Psychologically, I was trying to convince myself that I was getting better and the pain was not as strong as in the past days. However, I was only fooling and deceiving myself. I wonder if you have ever deceived yourself?

Finally, after six weeks of living with pain, one of my dearest and close friends convinced me to go to the V.A. hospital. She, and her husband, would drive down to my home from Lewisburg every day to take care of my cats. And, also, my friend, Anne found someone who would drive me to the V. A. hospital. I finally surrendered.

However, when the V. A. hospital initially examined me, they discovered that my right hip was shattered in pieces. And my right leg was two inches shorter than my left leg. The hospital would not operate and replace my hip. And so, I was transferred to another hospital to have the operation. The surgeon who, eventually, performed the operation was not happy because I had done unnecessary damage to my hip and walked for six weeks with a hip that was in pieces. And, he had to extend my right leg to its natural length to be even with my left leg so I could walk without a limp.

If I could leave a very important gift of my legacy with anyone who knows me or reads this book, that gift would be that we never walk alone. After my very serious hip replacement, God allowed me to walk again. And then, after recovering from my coma and stroke, when I was told that I would never walk again, I found the inner faith and strength to put one foot in front of the other foot and walk into the future.

Now, on clear days, I physically walk, at least, one hour a day. Most of the time, physically, I push myself to walk an hour and a half. And I know that I am not walking alone because I am talking to my parents, my Aunt "Mimi", my wife, Sharon, and my God.

See, now I believe that I have an inner consciousness of God. I have complete trust and faith in God. And that trust and faith is why I need to leave a legacy. I believe that I will never be afraid again because of my inner consciousness of God. And, I believe that no matter what happens to me, in my life, I will always be safe in God's hands. And that belief is a major part of my legacy to everyone who knows me or who reads this book. Just remember the definitions of a legacy. It is "the long-lasting impact of particular events, actions, etc. that took place in the past or in a person's life".

As I begin to think about how to end this chapter, I need to think about what people will think about me, especially my friends, when my mortal life comes to an end. What were my contributions to this life? What will I be remembered for after I am gone? Will I have left a lasting footprint that will be remembered by those people whose lives I have touched? Do you ever ask yourself those questions in the quietness of your day or night?

After returning to this life after the death of a coma, I realized that my biological clock was ticking and my time to live was not as long as I thought it was when I existed in my other life. See, when I was in a coma, I believed that I was only 55 years of age. I had to be convinced that, in this life, I was really 74 years old.

Realizing my mortality, I began to think about my life. What had I done in my life? What do I regret? What do I have to be thankful for in my life? What mistakes have I made along the way? What have been the moments of happiness and joy in my life? What have been my accomplishments and achievements? What will be the consequences of my past actions? Will my consequences outlive me? What is the summation of my past choices, decisions, and actions? How can I improve the quality of my life in the time that I have remaining in this life? I wonder if you have ever asked yourself those questions.

I believe that everyone leaves a legacy, whether or not they plan or intend to leave one. And I also believe that everything we say or do could leave an imprint of our lives on those people who have been part of our lives. And so, I believe that as long as there is breath within our bodies, there will always be an opportunity to leave other people a rich legacy of hope.

In the end, if there is one legacy that I could leave to everyone, it would be the hope that I have in God for my eternal life. Every day, I believe that I need to live as if that one day was my last day on this earth. Then, I need to reflect on what I could bring to Heaven. And maybe the only answer I could have is how I lived my life down here on earth.

Always believe in yourself, believe in the power of God, and believe that you can accomplish anything if you follow your dreams.

Chapter 3:
"THE MEANING OF LIFE"

(A Theological Perspective)

"The end of life is not to be happy, nor to achieve pleasure and avoid pain, but to do the Will of God, come what may.)

(The Reverend Doctor Martin Luther King, Jr., minister and activist)

In my life, I have known many people who were not happy with their lives, who wished that they had never been born, who questioned why they were born, who thought that their lives were not worth living, who felt as if they had wasted their lives, and, at times in my life, I have had those same thoughts and feelings.

I have lived with people who were homeless, abused in many ways, and addicted to various forms of drugs. I was a serious alcoholic for almost twenty-five years and, on several occasions, considered suicide, especially when I was living undercover in drug groups and organized crime as I questioned if what I was doing was worth living.

As I reflected on this chapter of my life, the lyrics to "WASTED DAYS" by Bruce Springsteen and John Mellencamp suddenly came into my mind. Think about the words:

"How many summers still remain,
Who is counting out these last remaining years,
How many minutes do we have here?

Wasted days,
Wasted days,
We watch our lives just fade away to more wasted days.

How much sorrow is left to climb,
How many promises are worth the time?
And who on earth is worth our time,
Is there a heart here that I can call mine?

How can a man watch his life go down the drain,
How many moments has he lost today,
And who among us could ever see clear?
The end is coming,
It is almost here.

Now, when you think about the words to those lyrics, released in September of 2021, by John Mellencamp and Bruce Springsteen, the message about the meaning of life within the words is both philosophical and theological. After all, we are all mortal beings and, eventually, the end will come and for many of us, it is almost here. The question is how much of our precious lives do we want to waste? See, each one of our lives is very precious. Each one of your lives is a precious gift from our Creator, our Maker, our God.

See, my whole perspective on the meaning of life, especially my life, was changed when I was returned to this life from a coma by God. I realized how precious my life is and how quickly, without warning, my life can be taken away.

I keep thinking about that uneasy passage of scripture in our Holy Christian Bible from Saint Paul to the Thessalonians:

"For when they say, 'Peace and safety, then suddenly destruction comes upon them, as labor pains upon a pregnant woman. And they shall not escape. But you, brethren, are not in darkness so that this day should overtake you as a thief. You are all sons (and daughters) of the day. We are not of the night nor darkness." (1 Thessalonians 5: 2-5)

I admit and confess that after I returned to this life from the darkness of my coma, I was angry at God for a while. Although I was alive, I realized that I had lost a year and a half of my life. However, as I continued to reflect on the reason for what had happened to me, I grew more thankful to God.

See, I now realize that God gave me a very unique experience that most people never acquire in life. And, yes, suddenly, and without warning, I was taken into another world, as if a thief in the night had taken my life. And, although I lived in the "shadows" of another world for some time, I remained in the "Light" of God because I would see, very clearly, my future in Eternity. In the reality of an unreal life, I was never in the darkness of the night. I was in the light of the dawning, the beginning, of a new day and a new life.

As I reflect on this chapter, I have to wonder why I wrote my second book, "DARK SOUL", years before I went into a coma. The title is so appropriate for the way my life was most of my life before my coma. For many years, I lived in the darkness of the shadows because of what I did as a police officer and undercover detective. And my actions caused my soul to become as black as the night. Then, God brought Sharon into my life and I could finally see and experience a bright new meaning for my life. Sharon finally taught me how to live and love life.

As I write at the beginning of my Introduction of "DARK SOUL", the book is an exploration into my soul. It was written as a journey into the darkness of my soul in quest of finding my way through the wilderness of my life. And I refer to a 2002 movie titled "WE WERE SOLDIERS" about the first major battle of the Vietnam War with members of The Seventh Calvery, almost like General Custer's last stand at the Little Bighorn so many years ago in 1876. This movie was about their battle in the Drang Valley, which would be known as "The Valley of Death". See, I now believe that God took me into my personal "Valley of Death" in a coma so that I could come alive again, tell my personal story about finding my way through the darkness, and truly appreciate the "Meaning of Life". Now, I understand why we have to experience death in order to understand and appreciate the meaning of life.

In the second chapter of my book, "DARK SOUL", titled "The Dichotomy of The Soul", I discuss how we can see the beauty and positive light that we can find in the darkness of painful losses in life if we can understand the connection between good and evil, good and bad, in a rational way. Then, we can, hopefully, understand how our tragedies in life can result in positive consequences. See, just as in the words of Holy Scripture found in 1 Peter, verse 9, in my coma, God called me "out of darkness and into His marvelous Light. Case in point, my coma has given me a more positive understanding of the "Meaning of Life" in a theological perspective.

And so, at this stage of your journey, I wonder if you have ever thought about the meaning of life or, specifically, have you ever reflected on the meaning of your personal life?

There have been many books written on "The Meaning of Life". The topic has been discussed and defined in several ways: Culturally, Philosophically, Ethically, Metaphysically, and Scientifically.

Basically defined, without a Theological perspective, "The Meaning of Life" can be described as when something or a series of events happen in our life for a reason. It is all about understanding how things fit together. Now, that might be a very simplistic definition of a complex issue.

However, "The Meaning of Life" can also be defined as having a purpose in life and understanding that specific purpose. It is the existence of goals and aims in your life. It could describe why you are alive because you are destined to do something or accomplish something in your life. Basically, it could outline your personal "Mission Statement".

And, in reality, your "Meaning in Life" could simply mean that your life matters, that you have a sense of direction, or what value and sense of worth you place on your life.

As I reflect on the meaning and purpose of this chapter, I think about the previous definitions of "The Meaning of Life". And I am drawn to the description of a personal "Mission Statement". At this stage of the journey that I call "Life", I have come to the realization and understanding that God saved my life and returned me from the death of a coma because I still have a mission in this life. I believe that I am destined to accomplish some goal that I still have not achieved, although, I still do not know what that goal is at this time.

And so, as I reflect on why I began to write this book, I now see this story as becoming my "Mission Statement". This book is part of my legacy and it will be my "meaning and purpose" for the remainder of my life until God gives me an "Expiration Date" and my mission will be complete. I believe that this book is the "Meaning of Life" for my life.

This chapter is forcing me to reflect on my life at the age of 77 years. I have to smile when I think about my journey, especially the early years. And, yes, I have lived a life that most people can only imagine. And, maybe, most people would not want to live the life that I have experienced. However, when I think about the meaning of my life, there are a couple of chapters in the book of my life that I would have changed or not written. I have done things that are either too painful to talk about or if I did write about some of the things I did, I would be in prison. And, now, at this stage of the journey, I have to confess that I am envious of husbands and wives who have celebrated twenty, thirty, or forty years of love together. I never had or will ever have that gift of togetherness.

However, keep in mind, that this chapter is focused on "The Meaning of Life" from a theological perspective. And so, let us return to our opening quote by the Reverend Doctor Martin Luther King, Jr. "The end of life is not to be happy, nor to achieve pleasure and avoid pain. But to do the Will of god, come what may."

At this stage of my life, or I should state, now, at the beginning of my new life, I confess that the early years of my past life, I did things that I admit were against the Will of God. I took lives and I really did not care about my life. For me, life had very little meaning or value. I had fun and pleasure, at times; however, that pleasure was only temporary. And, in reality, I did not care if I lived or died.

And I have to confess that I was never a sincere supporter of Reverend Doctor Martin Luther King, Jr. However, the meaning of the words found within this quote is very true and important in my life, at this stage, as I walk toward the end of my life and reflect on my past. I guess that I have a new point of view on the road ahead.

I agree with Doctor King, that the end of my life is not to

achieve pleasure or avoid pain. God knows that I have a lot of pain. God knows my health conditions and I realize that I need to live with pain if I want to live. I am truly thankful and grateful to God that I came out of the coma with a strong and sound mind and memory. I can think clearly and God has given me the gift of creating this legacy.

I also agree with Reverend Martin Luther King, Jr. that the end of my life is "to do the Will of God, come what may". See, I believe those words are the key to Doctor King's message and the meaning and purpose for my life, at this point, come what may happen in my future.

I believe that my God knows how my life will come to an end and when my "Expiration Date" will come due and my "Shelf Life" will be out of date. I cannot state that time. And so, I need to live each new day in a state of preparedness, a state of readiness.

Again, the focus of this chapter is to see in the light of "The Meaning of Life" from a theological perspective, that is, from the light of the answer found in the Holy Scripture outlined in the Holy Christian Bible.

As I researched Holy Scripture to support my theological perspective, I began to feel like I was back in seminary, working on a thesis for graduation. However, I hope you, the reader, do not feel that way as I attempt to defend my perspective.

Now, I truly believe that the "Meaning of Life", according to my Christian faith is ultimately found in the life of my Savior, Jesus Christ. See, in the life of Jesus Christ, we find our personal identity, our origin, our meaning and purpose, and our destiny, all given to each one of us with new hope for a better life.

Theologically, the "Meaning of Life" is rooted in the belief that we are beloved children of God, to reflect the Glory of God, to walk in His love, and to do His Will in our personal lives. That definition reflects the meaning of Doctor Martin Luther King, Jr. in his quote to us.

Our theological beliefs tell us that we are uniquely created by God, with natural talents and abilities to accomplish good works which God has called each one of us to do. (Ephesians 2:10, the Holy Christian Bible).

From a theological perspective, life is a process of growth and understanding the Power of Jesus Christ in our lives. It is, then for us, to believe that in Jesus Christ, we are constantly growing into a new creation of God if we can wait with faith. And so, "The Meaning of Life", then, becomes a continuous time of "becoming" the person that God intended us to be at the time of our birth. See, just as in my salvation from a coma, my past life is gone. And now, I have become a new creation, knowing and believing that Jesus Christ has saved me and lives within me. The sins and transgressions of my youth and past life have been forgiven. Now, I am a new person, a new creation, with a new life, as I wait to return to Eternity. (2

Corinthians 5:17, The New King James Version of the Holy Christian Bible)

"The Meaning of Life" from a theological perspective is to believe with a strong and deep faith in God, even when we have difficulty understanding the problems that we are confronted with in our mortal lives. See, in those times of uncertainty, we need to live with the eternal values of Faith, Hope, Love, and Belief that, even in the darkest hours, we are a reflection of God. We need to have a powerful faith in our Creator and believe in the Word and Work of God with the belief that Jesus Christ truly is the Word of God. (1 Corinthians 13:13, 2 Corinthians 3:18, John 1:1, The Holy Christian Bible)

In the end, from a theological perspective, "The Meaning of Life" is to prepare ourselves for a life beyond this existence. See, we must believe that there is something beyond our earthly life that God has placed in our human hearts and minds. We need to believe that our Creator is always in control, even in times when we cannot always control or understand the moment or the experience. (Ecclesiastes 3:11, The Holy Christian Bible)

After all, what really matters in our life is our reverence and obedience to God. And so, always trust in God, no matter what will happen throughout all the highs and lows of your life. See, the "Meaning of Life", in this life, is living in Faith,

Trust, Truth, Peace, Love, and Joy through the work of God's Spirit in our life. (Romans 14:17, The Holy Christian Bible)

Always keep in mind that life here on earth is a journey of our transformation to become more like Jesus Christ, the One who delivered us from evil, sin, and death until that glorious day that will come when we will live eternally with God and Jesus Christ in Heaven.

Chapter 4:
"SEASONS IN THE SUN"

"You cannot leave a footprint that lasts if you are always walking on tiptoe."

(Marion Blakey)

As I reflected on the quote by Marion Blakey, I thought about my life. All my life, I viewed myself as being shy and introverted. However, as I think about the journey of my life, at this stage, as my life goes into the "Winter" season, I can understand that the "footprints" that I made were more like "tripping" or stumbling or falling into situations and not intentionally "tiptoeing through the tulips" of experiences or situations.

I can honestly admit that I have always been very shy. As I stated earlier in this book, I could never talk to girls in school. I never dated or went to school dances. And to this day, I still cannot dance and I am too old to learn new tricks. However, as I reflected on my life in preparation for this chapter, I discovered that being shy is not the same as being an introvert.

See, by definition, an introvert is "a person whose personality is typically reserved or a quiet person who tends to be introspective and enjoys spending time alone". I have never been comfortable in large groups or at parties. And when I reflect on my years in parish ministry, I confess that I was always very nervous every Sunday morning before I began my sermon. I never enjoyed being the "center of attention". So, maybe that was why I was so good undercover in narcotics, drug groups, and organized crime associations.

Even to this day, I do not enjoy being around groups of people and I tend to alienate myself from social gatherings and events. My friends cannot understand why I choose not to socialize. However, I have always felt uncomfortable around people. Maybe, my personality is associated with the fact that I was an "only child". However, I still reflect on the journey of my life and I am amazed at all the "footprints" that I have made in life.

"SEASONS IN THE SUN" is an adaptation of an original song, "Le Moribond" (The Dying Man) that was written and recorded by Belgian singer-songwriter Jacques Brel in 1961. The lyrics were rewritten by Rod McKuen in 1963. The original lyrics tell the story of a dying man's farewell and goodbye to his loved ones as he was dying of a broken heart. As I researched this song, I reflected on my life after my wife, Sharon, died. As I write these words, I have to stop and think about my life with Sharon.

"SEASONS IN THE SUN" was recorded, again, in 1964 by The Kingston Trio. And, I am old enough to remember that group when they were popular during the "Hootenanny" period of folk music. However, Terry Jacks released the rendition of this very sentimental song that is the center and focus of this chapter in 1973. In his rendition, Terry Jacks dedicated this classic to his friend who was dying.

In his lyrics, Terry Jacks describes his friend as acknowledging the rights and wrongs of his actions in life as he passes away peacefully. I can only hope and pray that I will pass away peacefully when my time comes on my final day. All I ask of God is to take my spirit and my soul to where my mother, father, Aunt Mary, and my wife, Sharon, are in Eternity. My wish is to spend Eternity with them forever.

Now, please take a couple of minutes and reflect on the message of "SEASONS IN THE SUN" sung by Terry Jacks:

"We had joy, we had fun
We had Seasons in the Sun.
But the hills that we climbed
Were just seasons out of time.

Goodbye my friend, it is hard to die
When all the birds are singing in the sky.
Now that Spring is in the air
Pretty girls are everywhere.
Think of me and I will be there.

Goodbye papa, please pray for me
I was the black sheep of the family.
You tried to teach me right from wrong
Too much drink and too much song.
Wonder how I got along.

Goodbye Michelle
You gave me love and helped me find the sun.
And every time that I was down
You would always come around
And got my feet back on the ground.

Goodbye Michelle, it is hard to die
When all the birds are singing in the sky.
Now that Spring is in the air
With flowers everywhere.
I wish that we could both be there.

We had joy, we had fun
We had Seasons in the Sun.
But the stars we could reach
Were just starfish on the beach."

As I take some time to reflect on those lyrics, the words become increasingly painful to me as I think about my legacy and the end of my life. Honestly, I did have joy and fun in my life. However, I also had many painful, dark, and depressing times because of all my losses. Sadly, at this phase or moment in time for me, because I am alone, the painful memories overshadow the joyful periods in my life.

When I reflect on the words from Terry Jacks as he sings the lyrics of goodbye to his friend, I think about my blood brother, P. J. Werner. He was more than my partner in narcotics. P. J. taught me how to survive undercover. He taught me how to ride a motorcycle when I was going undercover with the Pagans motorcycle gang. On the night that we cut our wrists in a 7-11 store and blended our blood, we were bonded together forever. However, I thought that my wrist was going to need medical attention after we sterilized our cuts by pouring Yago Sangria wine on our wounds.

And yes, just as in the lyrics, pretty girls were everywhere in our lives. However, P. J. and I did a lot of interesting undercover work and I was introduced to people that I could only imagine knowing. People who would have had no problem killing me. The night that P. J. died changed my life.

There were many nights when I would go to P. J.'s grave with a bottle of Yago Sangria wine in a brown paper bag and talk to my brother. I would pour a glass of Yago into a paper cup and sit it near his headstone. For me, those moments would be like the endless hours that just the two of us would drive aimlessly around in our undercover van and just talk about life. We did not trust anyone, not even the other members of our unit. I will go to my grave with the secrets that P. J. shared with me and the secrets that I shared with him. We called our van "The Sea Witch" because P. J. had a mural of a naked girl riding on a surfboard on both sides of the van. P. J. Werner was my brother and will always be with me.

When I read the lyrics that begin with "Goodbye Papa", I become very emotional and sad. I think about all the times when I knew that my parents prayed for me. I am so very thankful that God blessed me with a mother, father, and aunt who loved me. I could never have hoped for parents who loved me more and unconditionally.

I know that my mother and father tried to teach me right from wrong; however, I also believe that, at times, I disappointed them. I caused them a lot of grief. I think they constantly worried about me.

I will never forget the time when I almost burned down our home. My father was tending bar that day at Doc Harrison's Tavern and my mother and Aunt Mimi were there with him. I was only a young boy. However, I was home alone. At that stage of life, I had a fascination with cigarette lighters. On that day, when I was playing in the house, I found an old German cigarette lighter that worked. I lit it. And then, I did not know how to put out the flame so I threw the burning lighter into a trash can that was filled with papers.

Of course, the flame created a fire. Not knowing what to do and afraid of starting a fire in the house, I carried the burning trash can through the house and took it outside. It had snowed the night before and there were several inches of snow on the ground. So, I threw the flaming trash can in the snow to put out the fire. I could have burned myself. Then, very nervously, I walked alone, to Doc Harrison's Tavern because I knew that my parents would find the burned trash can and the mess outside.

My mother, father, and Aunt Mimi were surprised to see me. When I confessed what I did, I expected to get physically punished. However, my parents did not even yell at me. They were just thankful that I did not get hurt or burned in the fire. I never played with cigarette lighters again.

I also will never forget stealing quarters several times from a gallon bottle full of money that my uncle had stored in our home. I used the money to take the bus to Annapolis. I knew my parents realized that the amount of silver coins was going down. However, they never confronted me. But then, I do not believe they ever knew that for a long period of time, when I was in the seventh grade, every month, I would steal a Playboy Magazine from the drugstore on my walk home from school.

However, I believe my parents really worried and were concerned about me when I was an alcoholic. I was arrested six times for Driving While Intoxicated and one time for Walking While Intoxicated while carrying a concealed deadly weapon. I was a licensed private investigator and I had a permit to carry a semi-automatic pistol. However, it was hanging out of the back pocket of my pants. By the Grace of God, I never went to prison. However, I did lose my driver's license for a year because of my first arrest when I drove my car into a used car lot and struck eight cars that were for sale.

So, I believe that I was the "Black Sheep" of the family out of all my cousins. However, I accomplished and experienced so much in life. And, although I never had the opportunity to say "Goodbye" to my mother, father, and Aunt Mary, I know that I will see them again, in Eternity, in Heaven.

And then, I really have tears in my eyes when I reflect on the lyrics that begin with "Goodbye Michelle". However, I have changed the name to "Sharon". Although I did have the gift of saying goodbye to Sharon and whispering in her ear, several times that I loved her before we had to turn off the machines, I believe, deep within my mind and heart that I will be with Sharon again in Eternity when my life comes to an end here on earth. See, in my coma, Sharon was there with me. I know that I will live forever in Eternity, in Heaven, with Sharon.

As I continue to reflect on the lyrics by Terry Jacks, when he sings about Michelle giving him love, helping him to find the sun, seeing birds in the sky, and believing Spring is in the air with flowers everywhere, that is the vision that I will always have of Sharon in my mind. See, my most loving memory of the six and one-half years that I was destined and blessed to live with Sharon was watching her create beautiful flower gardens.

Sharon was brilliant. However, she never had the opportunity to use her degree in Psychology, because of the abuse she suffered from her first husband. When we had a home built on a very beautiful area of ground in Northumberland where we could see the river on a clear day, Sharon would spend almost every nice day outside, working in the soil, and planting flowers. It was on those days when I would look out of my office window from the second floor of our home and just smile as I watched Sharon work her magic in the ground. Planting, growing, and creating new life in the growth of beautiful flowers was her therapy. I was ordering so much topsoil and mulch that I had to buy a pickup truck to save money. Sharon's flower gardens were planted all around our home. The neighbors would bring their friends to see Sharon's creations. And, although Sharon could never tell me that she loved me, I still have the two precious cards that she gave me where she wrote: "I love you".

Sharon died on April 25, 2005. Years later, after my father passed away in 2014 when I was alone, I would walk along the Susquehanna River in Dalmatia and see Sharon's reflection in the water. Then, I would smile and be at peace because I would think of the Springtime when Sharon would be working her magic in the soil and I would reflect on the only woman that I had truly ever loved in my life, knowing we would be together again, in the future.

Now, remember, the focus of this contribution is all about leaving a legacy. And so, again, I return to my old Brooklyn Park High School Literary Arts Magazine, "REFLECTIONS", from 1964. The essay is titled "AN ACQUAINTANCE". It was written by an extremely gifted member of our class when she was a junior in high school. I do not know if Christine Schoenemann is still living in this lifetime. However, her legacy still lives. Here is her offering. Remember, Christine was only 17 years of age when she created this legacy.

"The life of every human being in this congested world of ours is a fantastic maze of acquaintances. How often do you hasten past a person - a stranger - and think nothing of it? He is just a distant blot, someone apparently unimportant to your cluttered life. Then he smiles at you, and you are thrilled at the sensation your entire person feels - like the warm glow of sunshine within your heart. Who knows that in time this seemingly insignificant person may constantly be on your mind?

Then, one day, this blurred spot in your vision clears and becomes a part of your being. You converse, you enjoy, and you love. You realize how fortunate you were in meeting this person and you pray that the hour when you must part will never come.

All too swiftly that dreaded moment overtakes you, leaving a void within your frustrated heart. As the tedious days march slowly by the window of your mind you find yourself clinging to sweet memories and longing for just one more chat with that friend now so far away.

Then your spirit soars and your head overflows with love, for he has conveyed his fondness for you within a letter, and this once unimportant person becomes your most treasured acquaintance."

I have read Christine's essay from 1964 several times since I selected it to be included in this legacy. Each time I read it, I had to smile as I reflected on my journey with Sharon, the love of my life.

See, in the beginning, my image of Sharon was only a fantasy, a "whim", a sudden desire when I read her description in the newspaper "personals". For some reason, the way Sharon described herself really appealed to me. I had never seen Sharon; however, I was immediately attracted to her.

The first night we met, I knew that I was in love with Sharon. At the end of the night, I thanked God that my life had, now, been joined with Sharon's life. I was truly fortunate to meet Sharon.

And then, for the next six and one-half years, my love for Sharon became stronger as her health became weaker. We both knew and understood that Sharon would die soon. However, I never could accept the reality of losing Sharon. But I knew that her life or death was not my decision. And all the prayers and lighting of candles that I offered up to God would not change the reality of losing Sharon in this lifetime.

Now, I can only live with the memories of the years that I was blessed with Sharon's life in this lifetime. They were not all good years or happy times. Sharon suffered from severe mood swings and would not talk to me for days at times. However, when I would look out my office window and watch Sharon work her magic in the soil, creating life with flowers, I knew that she was at peace, if only for a brief period of time and I would smile. Now, all I have are the memories, photographs, and two cards that she wrote to me that I will treasure until the day I die of this life and find Sharon again, in Heaven, and live with her for Eternity.

However, I know that Sharon still lives with me in this life because I believe that she rides with me every time I drive the bright yellow Volkswagen Beetle that I bought for her in 2003. Sharon sits next to me and we talk about life and living as I thank Sharon for watching over our VW Beetle as it sits outside in the parking lot.

See, Sharon truly has left a "footprint" in my life as we, both, still walk together into the sunshine, into the future of my legacy.

Chapter 5:
"TURN! TURN! TURN!"

"Immortality is to live your life doing good things and leaving your mark behind."

(Brandon Lee, actor)

Immortality, from a philosophical or religious perspective, is defined as "the indefinite continuation of the mental, spiritual, or physical existence of a human being. The continued existence of an immaterial soul or mind beyond the physical death of the body."

As I reflect on our beginning quote by Brandon Lee, I would rather think of my personal immortality in the way he defines the process. That is, to basically live my life doing good things, doing good work, and leaving my "mark" behind when my physical body comes to an end in this life.

However, I have to confess that, in my past life, before my coma, I did not live my life always doing good things or good work. So, maybe, that is why God has given me a second, or final, opportunity to leave my "mark" behind in a good way as I reflect on the legacy that I hope to give people to remember me.

"TURN! TURN! TURN!" is a song that was originally written by Pete Seeger in 1959. The subtitle is "To Everything There Is A Season". Primarily, the lyrics are from the first eight verses of the Third Chapter found in the Book of Ecclesiastes from the Old Testament of The Holy Christian Bible.

Originally released in 1962 as "TO EVERYTHING THERE IS A SEASON" by a folk group known as The Limeliters, "TURN! TURN! TURN!" became a hit song in 1965 when it was released again by a folk-rock group known as The Byrds.

Now, please, take a couple of moments to reflect on some of the lyrics and think about your personal life:

"To everything, Turn, Turn, Turn, there is a season Turn, Turn, Turn, and a time to every purpose under Heaven.

A time to be born, a time to die.
A time to plant, a time to reap.
A time to kill, a time to heal.
A time to laugh, a time to weep.

A time to build up, a time to break down.
A time to dance, a time to mourn.
A time to cast away stones.
A time to gather stones together.

A time to love, a time to hate.
A time of war, a time of peace.
A time you may embrace.
A time to refrain from embracing.

A time to gain, a time to lose.

A time to rain, a time to sow.

A time for love, a time for hate.

A time for peace, I swear it is not too late"

See, for me, I believe that for everything in life, now, there is a "season" and a purpose. And I pray that the time is not too late for me.

As I write this chapter, I reflect on the time changes that we go through in America twice a year. The times when we "spring forward" in the Springtime of the calendar year, and "fall backward" in the Fall of the year. I know that there are times in our lives when we lose time, but, then we can make up time with the clocks on the wall. However, it is very difficult to make up time with our "biological clocks" as we reflect on the "cycle" of our lives.

As I continue to reflect on what I hope to be my legacy as I exist in this season of my life that I am living in, the "Winter" of my years, I return to my priceless two issues of "REFLECTIONS".

Within the 1965 issue of my high school literary arts magazine, I found a short poem that was written by one of my classmates, Rose Downey. I have not seen or talked to Rose since we graduated in 1965. I do not know if Rose is still alive in this world; however, her legacy lives on with the words that she wrote in "FOLDS OF BLACK MIST". As I reflect on her poem, I understand, appreciate, and realize the reason why my two issues of "REFLECTIONS" were saved by the people who moved my personal possessions when they did not pack my expensive research books. They did not know me. See, these publications are priceless to me, just like the words from my classmates are priceless in the legacies that they leave the world. My hope is that the books that I create will be part of my legacy long after my spirit is lifted up and into heaven for Eternity.

Now, please, take another couple of moments to reflect on "FOLDS OF BLACK MIST" by Rose Downey:

"Three golden statues adorn my shelf, each representing a phase of my life.
The first is the morn, serene and calm as a blue-green pond, lapping gently in the early mist.
Its surface is disturbed only by falling dew.

Too soon, the morn gives way to day, displacing aimless pleasure.
And the brilliance of full sunlight glows through the busy hours.

The climax passes as noon, scarcely noticed, and the soft, silent shadows of twilight creep in,
Taking me by surprise.
They swathe me in caressing folds of black mist.
MIDNIGHT HAS COME."

When I read the poem by Rose Downey, my thoughts flashed back to the original song by Pete Seeger and The Limeliters, "TO EVERYTHING THERE IS A SEASON". I began to reflect on my own life and feel the aging process as my "biological clock" continued to tick toward the hour of "Black Mist" in the poem as I walked close to midnight in the "Winter" season of my mortal life. I have so much that I still hope to accomplish and so little time to do it. I wonder if you have ever felt this way and what you plan to do with the remainder of your life.

As I have said in the past, I see each new day as a lifetime. When I open my eyes in the morning, for me, it is like "Springtime". I feel "born again" at that moment in time and I thank God for one more day of life, hopefully. As my day passes through late morning and into the early afternoon hours, it is like I am passing into the "Summer" of my life. And then, as late afternoon and early evening come, I begin the "Fall" season of my day as I walk into the "Fold of Black Mist", the "Midnight of Winter" before I close my eyes to this day of my life and fall into a deep sleep.

See, in a very poetic way, I believe that is how Rose Downey described the final season of life when she was only eighteen years of age. That is the time when we realize that our life is almost at an end, when "the soft, silent shadows of twilight creep in" taking us by surprise. Rose truly described the "seasons" of life in her descriptions of the three golden statues that she found on her shelf, the "shelf" of her life at such a young age.

In 1969, Elizabeth Kubler-Ross, a Swiss Psychiatrist, defined what she believed to be the five stages of Grief. She described these stages as Denial, Anger, Bargaining, Depression, and Acceptance. As I reflect on my life, I acknowledge that I have gone through each one of those stages at different points in my life as I experienced losses. Significantly, the last stage was the loss of my wife, Sharon. After nineteen years, I still mourn the death of the only woman I have ever loved in this life and I have vowed never to fall in love again. In fact, in my mind, I am still married to Sharon and I wear her wedding ring on my left hand.

As defined by Elizabeth Kubler-Ross, the five stages, again, of Grief are

DENIAL - A point where life does not make any sense. When life has no meaning.

ANGER - When we ask ourselves, "Why Me?" I confess that I have been angry with God many times in my life, especially when Sharon was dying.

BARGAINING - I tried to "bargain" with God every week during Sharon's last days.

I would go to the Catholic church where we said our vows and light candles

I would pray to God to extend Sharon's life and shorten my life.

And then, I believed that my prayers did not matter and that God was not listening to me.

DEPRESSION - A feeling of emptiness. A declaration that the situation is over and gone.

A feeling that there is nothing to live for now. That is the way I felt when I had to make the decision to shut down Sharon's life support machines and let her life drift away.

I just wanted to withdraw from life and not associate with anyone unless I had to be with them. Fortunately, my mother and father were still alive.

ACCEPTANCE (the final stage) - A feeling that everything is going to be okay. It is coming to terms with a new "reality" of life and living. It means coming to a sense of peace and socializing again. I am still working on that stage. However, I am getting better because I am in the "Winter" season of my mortal life and I believe that I will be united with Sharon again soon.

At this stage of the journey, I have a very strong belief and Faith in God. This Faith is the result of my coma. To live with a powerful Faith in God is a very important part of my legacy for everyone. See there were many moments in my life when I doubted the presence of God in my life. There were times in my life during the years when I lived undercover in drug groups and organized crime that I prayed to God to take my life because I did not want to live with what I had done.

However, my will was not God's Will. And I had to live with my actions.

I believe that most of us have to live through the dark parts of our lives, the nights of our existence, the times of failure, when we deeply feel the struggles and the tragedies of life. However, now, I truly and honestly believe that in those moments of darkness, the sunshine and the brightness of a Spiritual Connection with God will show us the way to walk through the shadows.

Living, finally, in the last stage of Grief, which is Acceptance, I have come to a point of surrender in my life. I am finally at peace with my Higher Power, my Creator, my God. Now, I accept each new day as a joyful sunrise, a new gift from God. The darkness of the night has passed and I am alive in the brightness of a new day, even if the weather outside is cloudy, rainy, and full of storms.

And when I do my daily morning prayers, I begin each new day by putting away the old mistakes of yesterday. See, now I believe that God always offers me a fresh new start in life every day so that I can open my eyes one more time. I believe that God has forgiven me for my past mistakes and sins. I believe that God wants me to live a new life for today in preparation for tomorrow and an Eternal life in the future together with my wife, Sharon.

The "Winter" season is a time for "Reflection"; however, it is also a time for "Goodbyes". It is a time to reflect on our past and say "Goodbye" to those special people we loved and who loved us, the people who made a lifelong impact on our lives. For me, saying "Goodbye" to someone special has never been easy to do. To say "Goodbye", at times, can be the most difficult and painful part of living.

At this stage of my journey, I find myself reflecting on many friends who have died, especially, in their early lives. I think of friends who died not long after graduation from high school and I wonder "Why?". They had a lifetime to live. Several of my friends died in Vietnam. That war was such a waste of life. Then, I reflect on my blood brother, P. J. Werner, who died in the line of duty as a police officer. His death changed my life. And I wonder "Why?". Why was I blessed to live so long?

As I continue to write this journal about my legacy, I find that the contents of this book have created a mind of its own. Now, I return to that old high school literary magazine that has recorded the legacies of so many of my high school friends and classmates. Many of them are no longer alive in this lifetime.

In the 1964 issue of "REFLECTIONS", when I was a junior in high school, a young girl that I knew wrote a poem that reflects my thoughts today. The title of the poem is "DETHRONEMENT". Phyllis Jackson might not be physically alive today. However, her words will live forever, or, at least, as long as I have the magazine. Here is her offering to you.

"From the brown, bark-covered branch

I ventured, budding and blossoming slowly.

Each morning, I reached out to bathe myself in the sun.

I drank the soft rain to quench my thirst.

And daily I spat my breath into the air.

That Spring, then Summer, stepped aside to let Autumn reign.

I little cared.

But one Fall day, quite clear and bright, a shadow crept over me

And rustled me from my throne.

From the onset of Winter, I must escape,

So I danced with the rhythms of the wind.

Until I lay on the cold, wet ground.

My beautiful color has turned to brown.

AND NOW I AM DEAD."

As Phyllis Jackson depicts and paints a vivid picture of the life of a beautiful leaf on a tree, she describes my vision of the stages of life in the seasons of the year. As a seed, we come to life, after we are planted, and then we grow and blossom. However, sadly, eventually, our beautiful bodies decay and we die. How we live our lives and what we experience as we go and grow through the stages of life will create the person we are at the end of our existence in this lifetime.

In the next chapter, we will focus on the "heart" of this contribution and legacy. We will reflect on the first eight verses found in the third chapter of the Book of Ecclesiastes in the Old Testament of the Holy Christian Bible. Those verses are, primarily, the body of lyrics to "TURN! TURN! TURN!" by The Byrds and the central theme of this journal.

Chapter 6:
"A TIME FOR EVERY PURPOSE UNDER THE SUN"

"The great use of life is to spend it for something that will outlast it."

(William James, philosopher)

As I begin to reflect on this chapter, Spring has come and I can feel the warmth of renewal as I begin to take long walks, again, around Lewisburg after a long dark winter. As I pass the other people walking, I can see the freshness of their lives when they smile at me. It is as if the world is coming alive again. I feel like a new cycle of life is becoming awakened with the sounds of Spring. This is such a wonderfully healthy time of the year as the days grow longer with extended sunlife after we have moved the clocks ahead. The dark cold days and nights begin to give way to the fresh new sounds of Spring with the birds singing and there is a feeling of rebirth in the air, a cycle of new life has come around.

In my journey through the pages of this offering, I have included several poems from my old high school literary magazine, "REFLECTIONS". So, to lead into this chapter, I have found one more offering. The title of this poem is "AWAKENING". It is from the 1964 issue of the publication.

The poem was written by Myrna Boyd, a senior in the class one year ahead of me. I had never met Myrna and I do not know if she is still living in this lifetime. However, her words are still alive in her legacy. Now, please reflect for a couple of minutes on Myrna Boyd's "AWAKENING".

"SPRING

An awakening of the world,
When the earth's breast is warmed by glowing sunshine,
And young hearts dance joyously in sweet ecstasy,
Awakening to a new love.

SPRING

A renascence of the soul,
When life is again imbued (inspired) into the old and weary,
And a gleam of hope glistens in their shallowed eyes,
As inevitable death is seemingly forgotten.

SPRING

The dawning of days of roses,
When all nature blossoms and dons a veil of delightful greenery,
And God's world rests tranquility in a mode of elegant splendor,
Embellishing a tired earth."

In my view, I believe that the most reflective part of Myrna Boyd's poem is found in the second section as she describes "SPRING" as a "renascence of the soul". Renascence is basically describing something that has been in a stage of dormancy, a period of time when life has been temporarily stopped, as in the "Winter" season. And then, Springtime begins to bring everything back to life once again. As Myrna describes this growth process, suddenly, we feel "a gleam of hope" that lightens up our old dark nights and we come alive as we open our eyes to the birth of a new day. Then, for a short period of time, that could seem like a lifetime, the "inevitable death" is forgotten. We rise up and face the challenges of one more new day. However, we can also appreciate the joys and accomplishments of our work and goals.

As I stated earlier, within this journal of my journey, I have included several poems as references. Now, the focus of this chapter comes to life in the form of another poem. However, this poem is a very unique and powerful offering because it is written as Scripture in the Holy Christian Bible.

The "heart" of my chapter is found in the third chapter of The Book of Ecclesiastes from The Old Testament of The Holy Christian Bible. Now, for a couple of minutes, please reflect on the words found in verses 1-8 that have been translated from The New King James Version of the Bible.

"To everything, there is a season.
A time for every purpose under Heaven.

A time to be born,
A time to die.

A time to plant,
And a time to pluck what is planted.

A time to kill,
And a time to heal.

A time to break down,
And a time to build up.

A time to weep,
And a time to laugh.

A time to mourn,
And a time to dance.

A time to cast away stones,
And a time to gather stones.

A time to embrace,
And a time to refrain from embracing.

A time to gain,
And a time to lose.

A time to keep,
And a time to throw away.

A time to tear,
And a time to sew.

A time to keep silent,

And a time to speak.

A time to love,
And a time to hate.

A time of war,
And a time of peace."

As I stated earlier, Ecclesiastes, Chapter Three, verses 1-8 was written as a poem, in a unique way of depicting or presenting the stages of our lives, at times, as a series of paradoxes or contradictory perspectives, or points of view.

For example, the way I lived my life as an adult truly is a paradox, a contradiction, in the way my life was lived as a child and a very young boy.

If I had had the gift of observing the cycles or stages of my adult life before I graduated from high school, I would have never believed or imagined that I would have had the courage, or maybe the stupidity, to do the things I did and accomplish as an adult. See, the journey of my life truly has been a series of self-contradictory cycles of life that are honestly logically difficult to explain.

However, I lived through those cycles of life and I experienced many changes in my life since graduation from high school and venturing into the unknown in the years ahead of school, even when I had doubts about my creative abilities and faith in myself. I wonder if you have ever reflected on the cycles of your life and thought about what you have experienced, achieved, or failed to accomplish at different times.

See, the message of Ecclesiastes, Chapter Three, verses 1-8, from The Old Testament of the Holy Christian Bible was written long ago as a "reflection" of, and for, each one of our lives today. It is a reflection for us when we look in the mirror and see the lines on our faces. If we look deep enough, we can see and remember the cycles of our existence in the reflection on the nature of living our life in the past. And, maybe, we can also be able to see our lives in the future by reflecting on the way we are living today. See, everything we have done in the past, and everything we will do today will reflect on how we will live our lives in the future. Everything we do, or do not do, has a meaning and a purpose. And that statement is a major part of the legacy that I will leave behind when my "expiration date" comes due in this mortal life.

See, my hope is that you can take the time to reflect on the power of Faith, the power of Faith in God, and the power of faith in yourself. As I write these words of my legacy, I write with a strong and deep Faith in God to accept the reality of my life and to understand that the cycle of life, especially the cycle of my life, has always been part of a very intricate and specific plan of God. I believe that my Creator God directs every event that has ever happened in my life from Heaven Above.

I believe that every event under Heaven has an appointed time and everything that has ever happened in my life has mattered to me. Case in point, for example, the building of my garage.

Ever since my father passed away in 2014 and I inherited his home, a mobile home trailer, I had thought about building a garage next to the small structure to store special possessions, including my classic 1970 Chevrolet Chevelle and the 2003 Volkswagen Beetle that I had bought for my wife, Sharon, two years before she died. Well, finally, in 2020, I got a loan from the bank to build the garage. When the garage was finally finished, the structure was almost twice as big as my mobile trailer home.

I decided to sell my classic Chevrolet Chevelle because I did not want to drive it. Then, the event happened that was to change my life again. I went into a coma. Fortunately, I had sold the Chevelle. However, my home, garage, property, land, and all my personal possessions were sold at a Sheriff's Sale to pay for the bank loan that I had been granted to build the garage. When God returned me to this life after the death of my coma, the bank loan had been settled and I had lost my home. However, my Volkswagen was returned to me. And when my wallet was returned, I found the final payment for the Chevy Chevelle. However, I had to smile because the check had expired because it was dated two years earlier and I could not cash it. But, then, the amount was only $80.00.

See, the poem found in our Scripture lesson for this chapter is a reflection on the natural rhythm of life and living.

It describes the natural cycles of life by listing the nature of life and living which includes:

–   Birth and Death.

–   Killing and Healing.

–   Tearing Down and Building Up.

–   Weeping and Laughing.

–   Mourning and Dancing (think of the celebration of life at a funeral).

–   Accepting and Letting Go.

–   Loving and Hating (think about relationships and marriages).

–   Silence and Speaking.

See, this poem, found in the Scripture of Ecclesiastes, Chapter Three presents a foundation to live by and to leave a legacy. It describes the fundamental cycles of life that give our lives meaning and purpose. Think about it. If we could not experience death, we would not appreciate birth in a new life. If we could not have the ability to tear down the old structures of living, we could not have the gift of experiencing the joy and celebration of building up a new life. If we could not let go of the past, then we could not appreciate the acceptance of a new and better life in the future.

As I continue to reflect on the cycles of my personal life, I can see how the new stages of my life were created as the result of the previous stage or cycle. For example, my decision to enlist in the Air Force directly out of high school grew from my fascination with an old movie titled "THIRTY SECONDS OVER TOKYO", a movie produced in 1944, which was before I was born and you probably never heard of. However, I believe that I have lived a past life, even before I was born into this life. The movie was based on the historic retaliatory air strike against Japan four months after the bombing of Pearl Harbor. What fascinated me, primarily, about this true movie was the aircrews that volunteered for the mission, realizing that they might not live and return home to their families. Because of that movie, I wanted to go to Vietnam during the war.

However, now I understand that God had other plans for my life. Although I did join the Air Force, I was set back in basic training because I could not pass the physical training. When I did pass the obstacle course, my career field and assignment had been changed. I was, now, to become a Graphic Arts Illustrator and assigned to Washington, D.C. However, I finally did get my wish after I repeatedly requested transfers to Vietnam. Eventually, I was transferred to Taiwan and flew into Vietnam.

Because of my experience as a Graphic Arts Illustrator, the cycle of my life led me into a unique position as an

Illustrator for The Bureau of Customs in Washington, D.C. after the Air Force. But, I still was not happy.

See, God still had other plans for me. Eventually, I joined the Baltimore City Police Department and became involved in the police strike of 1974. That decision would lead me to resign from the Baltimore City Police Department and join the Anne Arundel County (Maryland) Police Department. As the cycle of my life continued, I would get involved with what I really wanted to do as a police officer when I was transferred into the Narcotics Unit and live undercover.

The cycle would revolve, again, when I was forced to resign from the police department, work as a licensed private investigator and, eventually, move to Pennsylvania and enter a Protestant seminary when I was Roman Catholic. It was at this point that God would save my life, again, in seminary because I was directed into treatment for my alcohol dependency.

I hope that you can see the patterns of the cycles of my life. I hope that you can appreciate and understand that the decisions and experiences that I have had in life have all led me to the next cycle, the next level of living. If I had not made certain decisions, at specific moments in time, I would not have been directed to make other more positive choices and, eventually, become the person and the writer that I am today as I leave my legacy for you.

I believe that the cycles of opportunities that were created for me directly resulted from decisions made in past cycles and have created who I am today. However, now, I also believe that God was directing and orchestrating every situation. See, in reality, each one of our lives is one continuous cycle in the cycle of life and living.

In the end, the goal of this chapter is to, primarily, focus on and present a descriptive definition of the cycle of life. This cycle of living is sort of a balance, a give and take, a process of gaining and losing.

We need to keep in mind that the events in our lives, the cycles of our lives and existence will happen. Maybe we cannot control all the events in our lives; however, the one thing that we can control in any event is our personal "perspective", our attitude toward the event, and our point of view of what is happening in our lives.

See, we need to remember that the difference between enjoying life and hating life stems directly from how we see life, our perspective or perception of our life.

Always understand and believe that each one of our lives will have a beginning and an ending. None of us chose when it was time to be born. We did not choose who would be our parents. We did not choose what race or nationality we would be born into. We did not choose what country we would be born in. God decided all those factors for us.

Now, our choice is to decide what to do with the remainder of our lives. Will we appreciate our life or will we hate our life? Will we be grateful that we were born?

Chapter 7:
"THE LEFT EYE"

"No legacy is so rich as honesty."

(William Shakespeare, playwright)

Bell's Palsy (or peripheral facial palsy) is caused by the swelling and inflammation of the nerve that controls the muscles on one side of the face. There is no known cause for this form of palsy. And it can occur more than one time in a person's life. When this palsy comes, half of a person's face will droop, your smile will be one-sided, and the eye on the affected side will resist closing. A person could have frequent headaches, loss of taste, dry eye, and an increased sensitivity to sound. However, this form of palsy is rare with less than 200,000 cases per year. Maybe, I was one of the lucky ones to have it.

Now, maybe you are wondering why I began this chapter with a description of Bell's Palsy because this book is all about leaving a legacy. Well, I developed Bell's Palsy after my coma and it has affected my physical sight. However, the lasting effects of this condition, although I am not really suffering from it now, have helped me to focus on my legacy and see more clearly within my soul.

However, I believe that I will have permanent minor residual issues, including a problem with my left eyelid not being able to open wide, which affects my vision, and the left side of my mouth that is raised higher than the rest of my mouth. But then, I still do feel very fortunate.

See, my condition that is affecting my physical sight has given me a new, deeper, and stronger inner vision. My physical sight limitation has actually allowed me to reflect on reminding me of an old quote by William Shakespeare who wrote: "The eyes are the windows to your soul". So, maybe I should have titled this chapter from the pen and mind of William Shakespeare, "YOUR EYES ARE THE WINDOWS OF YOUR SOUL".

See, even with a weak left eye, when I focus on my legacy, I can see more clearly into my soul as I live each day toward my final "expiration due date". The point to remember for this chapter is that Shakespeare's quote, "The eyes are the windows to your soul", suggests that a person's eyes are the "windows" into how we feel, what we think, and how we see ourselves. And that belief is a major reflection of my legacy.

Now, think about our opening quote for this chapter, also given to us by William Shakespeare. "No legacy is so rich as honesty". I have come to the realization that I have to be honest about myself as I reflect on the legacy that I hope to leave for other people.

As I reflected on Shakespeare"s words about our eyes being "the windows of the soul", I remembered a verse of scripture from The Holy Christian Bible, The Book of Acts,

Chapter 9, verse 18, "Immediately there fell from his eyes something like scales, and he received his sight at once, and he arose and was baptized". (The New King James Version).

In a very powerful way, as I reflect on my recovery and new life after returning from the death of a coma, I feel like I was able to rise up and begin a new life. Maybe God gave me a temporary form of palsy to lift the old "scales" from my eyes that I had been focusing on in the past and now I can see more clearly what I need to work on in the future.

So, now that we are focused on the "Windows of the Soul" after lifting the "scales" from my left eye, how do we define "Soul"?

Well, the Greek translation of "Soul" is "Psuche". This word almost sounds like the root word for "Psychology". However, "Psuche" can be translated as "breath, life, person, soul, or self".

The Holy Christian Bible teaches us that the "Soul" is defined as the symbol of LIFE. It is the spiritual or immortal part of a human being. The "Soul" of a human being is the "totality of the person as a center of life, emotions, feelings, longings, and thinking that can be only fully realized in union with God.

Now, I finally realize that after I opened my eyes and could see my life with a clearer vision, I felt that I had been given a new life with a closer relationship and personal union with God, my Creator.

See, in the Gospel of Matthew, Chapter 6, verses 22, 23, "The LAMP of the body is the EYE. If therefore your eye is good, your whole body will be full of light. But if your eye is bad, your whole body will be full of darkness. If therefore the light that is in you is darkness, how great is that darkness!". (The New King James Version, The Holy Christian Bible).

As I reflect on my new life, after my temporary illness of Bell's Palsy, following my coma, I truly do feel very fortunate for the palsy because the condition is rare, with less than 200,000 cases recorded in the United States every year.

Lately, I find myself wanting to take long walks on nice warm days as the time of Spring becomes warmer. However, as I walk, I also experience the film of the "scales" in my left eye return at times. Actually, both of my eyes fill with water and my vision becomes more blurry as I walk. I need to really watch the sidewalks because I do not want to trip and fall. As I think about my walking with blurry eyes, I have to smile because I can relate to the steps that I take on the rough sidewalks with the rough and dangerous steps that I have taken in my walk through life. And I do not want to trip and fall in life as I walk through the new life that God has granted to me.

See, I now know that when my left eye becomes blurry with film and water, I can stop and rest. Then, I can wipe the scales of water from both of my eyes and I can see more clearly again after I take a break from walking. And then I can stand up straight and continue my walk in life.

In the Gospel of Matthew, in the Holy Christian Bible, I can see the relationship to how our eyes are "the windows to our soul". Remember, the symbol of life IS the Soul.

Again, in Matthew, Chapter 6, verses 22 and 23, we can see that "the lamp of the body is the eye. If therefore your eye is good, then your whole body will be full of light. But if your eye is bad, then your whole body will be full of darkness. If therefore the light that is in you is darkness, how great is that darkness!".

See, if our eyes are healthy, then our whole body will be healthy. If our whole body is healthy, then we will be full of the light of life. See, our eyes truly are the "windows to our soul" because they can reflect to other people what our true thoughts, feelings, intentions, emotions, and characters are in our lives. Our eyes have the power of communication to others even in times when we do not say a word in response or reply to someone who will ask us how we are feeling.

As I walk the paths around Lewisburg, I have to smile as I pass people who are coming toward me in their walks. I smile when they smile to me and I wonder what they arre thinking about me as they pass me by in life. I am never dressed well. I wear the oldest, most worn clothing and old coat that I can find on my rack.

I wonder what the people who pass me on the trails think about my "identity" and how they view me when they pass me and smile. See, I walk with a limp from my stroke and I am always looking down to the ground. The people I pass in life do not know that I was told that I would never walk again. When they pass me, I think about my true and real "identity". And I realize that no one really knows the real "person" who I am inside. As I always say to people, "you never really know what the other person is thinking".

As I wrote in my second book, "DARK SOUL", for many people, the "inner person", the inner true "identity" of who a person perceives his or her self to be within their mind, psyche, or soul many times, does not always reflect the image that other people see in their interactions. And our reflection is not always an accurate perception of the other person or ourselves in relationships.

See, as I pass people along my walks through the remainder of my life, I realize that I have to always remove the "scales" from, not only my left eye, but from both of my eyes, so I can see other people more clearly and they can have a better reflection of my true identity.

See, I now, truly, understand and believe in the eternal life of my soul after God, my Creator, granted me a "rebirth", a "reincarnation", after returning me to this life after awakening from a coma and seeing Eternity for a brief period of time. In that way, God truly did give me a bright view from "the window of my soul".

In my last chapter, I focused on the many stages of the "cycles" of life. I indicated that in every cycle, there is always a "death" of a past cycle in order for the "birth" of a new stage or cycle of life to begin. The "death" of a past cycle can be extremely powerful in and to the way we see ourselves after each cycle. I am so very grateful for the cycle that I lived in during my coma because it gave me a new life and a bright new vision for my future in the next cycle of my life. I am also very thankful for my temporary vision with Bell's Palsy because it has allowed my life to become more visible to myself. It has shown me that I have lived with scales over my eyes for most of my life.

See, I believe the scales and cloudy film on my left eye is only a temporary vision of darkness. And when I stop and take the time to wipe my eyes clear of the darkness then I can see a vision of a bright new path to walk in life. The "window" is more clear and I can see a healthier soul as I walk toward my final "expiration due date" and when my "shelf life" has become out of date.

"I have found so much beauty in the darkness, as I have found so much horror in the light."

(Azereth Skivel)

I will always be grateful to God for giving me a new life after my coma. However, I will also always be thankful to God for returning my mind and memory to me so I can remember and reflect on the cycles of my life in the life that I lived before my coma. As you know, one of those dark cycles involved the years that I lived undercover in drug groups and organized crime associations. See, it was during those dark years that I became very proficient and skilled in the art of looking into the eyes of the "bad guys" that I was working against. I had to read their souls in order to win at the game and stay alive.

I have used the quote by Azereth Skivel in my second book, "DARK SOUL". I know the quote can be slightly fearful. However, please take a couple of minutes to study the words. When Skivel states that he has "found so much beauty in the darkness", I believe that image can be a positive reflection on life, even when our eyes are closed as we rest and sleep during the night. See, there is beauty in sleep. We need our sleep to rest during the dark hours of the night in order to prepare ourselves for the beginning of a new day, the dawning of a new day, a new life. When we sleep and rest in the darkness, we can block out everything that is troubling us. We can close our eyes to the pain and the pressure of the stressful situations that we face when we are awake. We can give our minds a rest to rejuvenate, revitalize, replenish, and restore our mental and physical strength in order to possibly and positively face the painful challenges of the new day. And when we wake up and open our eyes to a bright new day, hopefully, the "horrors" that we will face from the day before will be less painful.

As I begin to come to an end in this chapter that has been focused, primarily, on our eyes being "the windows to our soul", I also need to reflect on the need to see our "self-image" as we look into the "windows", the "mirror of our mind". How do we see ourselves when we remove the "scales" and the film from our eyes as we walk the paths of life that are in front of us in the future?

For me, I believe that I need to see a clear path and a clear road ahead as I walk through the days of my new life. I need to see a clear reflection when I look into the "mirrors" of my mind and soul as I prepare for my final "expiration due date". I need to reflect on and remember the paths that I have taken that have led me to the beginning of this bright new day and new life. And I need to understand and realize that I cannot turn back now.

The painful mistakes that I made in my past life, before the coma, need to be remembered only for the painful lessons that I have learned in the journey. I need to remember the darkness of the night before I went to sleep in my coma. Now, I have awakened to a bright new day that I will always cherish and thank God for my new life.

Chapter 8:
"LIVING THE DREAM"

"Carve your name on hearts, not on tombstones. A legacy is etched into the minds of others and the stories they share about you."

(Shannon Adler, author)

As I reflected on our beginning quote for this chapter, I remembered a young girl in our high school senior class. I always thought that she was one of the most beautiful girls in our class through the years in high school. However, I never had the courage to talk to her because I was so shy and afraid of girls.

When I saw her contribution to my old high school literary arts publication, "REFLECTIONS", from 1965, I knew that I had to include her thoughts and feelings in this journal about leaving a legacy. See, she carved her name in my heart, just like the words from our opening quote. So, I decided to open this chapter with her essay titled "DREAMS".

However, first, I took out my old senior class yearbook and opened it to the page to see her senior class photograph. I can still imagine her and dream about how beautiful she was in 1965. Although, I also had to smile when I looked at the picture of the boy next to her on the page. The last time that I saw John, I was arresting him for the murder of his best friend, another classmate of mine, when I was an undercover police detective in narcotics. Both John and this beautiful young girl were on the Academic track in high school. However, I guess they had different visions or dreams for their future lives.

Now, I will begin this chapter with a beautiful essay on "DREAMS" by Donna Marie Harryman. Sadly, I have recently learned that Donna died several years ago from cancer. However, Donna's legacy will live forever in the hearts and minds of the people who knew her and the stories that they will share about Donna Marie Harryman.

So, please take a couple of minutes and reflect on the words found in "DREAMS".

"Dreams are imaginations manifesting themselves in shapeless forms until we trample them into oblivion. Yet, they are patterns for our living and originators of our goals.

Dreams, too, are our hopes. They excite us into revelry, depress us into obscurity, or confuse and mystify us until we reach the point of frustration. At the same time, they are one of the most prominent aspects of life. During childhood, we envision ourselves as government employees, elected officials, or members of important professions, and from such inspiration, enhanced by education, we become such and have our realm of dreams become reality.

History has been shaped by the dreams of men. Rulers desiring improvements for their subjects undertake projects to satisfy this dream. An individual wants personal fame and directs all his energies toward satisfying his ambition. The first man to envision a journey into outer space was considered a fool, but his dream from yesterday has become today's reality. Thus, it seems that dreaming in major magnitude is more rewarding than dreaming in lesser ones.

The realization that all dreams cannot and will not come true is significant to our emotional lives. Frequently, what seems like failures may actually be maximum successes. However, we must not feel content, for minds permitted to regress are of little value. Our complacency can be a burden to others. Necessity teaches us that failure must be met by striving to catch the next seemingly abstract dream and transposing it into reality.

Dreams have no beginnings and no endings. Rather, they are endless structures, perpetually being built upon and renovated, while we tear down old portions and add new sections in a never-ending cycle. We get momentary pleasure when our dreams culminate in success. But soon we find ourselves setting higher goals and dreaming new dreams. And from them, comes all the progress in the world."

As I read Donna Harryman's insightful understanding, very perceptive examination, and colorful descriptions of Dreams, I continued to think about the mind of the beautiful young girl that I never had the courage to approach in my high school class all those years. Not only was Donna physically very beautiful but I, now, realize that she had a beautiful mind.

My hope is that Donna Marie Harryman was allowed to live her dreams in the years that she was alive in this world. I hope and pray that all her dreams came true.

Now, contrast Donna's amazing essay with my simple contribution to the same issue of "REFLECTIONS" and you can imagine what I was dreaming about in 1965. Who would have dreamt or dreamed that in my later years, I would create and publish two magazines and, then, write and publish five books?

Again, here is my award-winning contribution to my senior year publication in high school.

"I AM YOUTH!
I am Youth!
I am impulsive.
I act without thinking.
I live from week-end to week-end.
I exist from one summer to another.
I love music, speed, and the opposite sex.
I enjoy coming to school.
I dread exams.
I am Youth!

So, now you can see where my mind and dreams were in 1965. However, I must confess that I was not living all my dreams at that time.

Now, let's take a couple of minutes to reflect on Donna Harryman's "DREAMS". For my life, I agree that Dreams "are patterns for our living and originators for our goals". Those thoughts are the primary reasons why I chose "LIVING THE DREAM" for the title of this chapter. I can honestly state that I have accomplished almost every goal that I set for myself in this life. I have ventured into every profession and occupation that I ever dreamed of having and working in the journey of my life. Although, I must also confess and admit that I was very fortunate to live through several of my "dream" adventures.

As Donna Harryman states, "Dreams, too, are our hopes, they are one of the most prominent aspects of life, and our realm of dreams become reality". See, each one of us should live with dreams for a better life. Without dreams, our lives can be such a waste of time and life. And the hope of, at least, some of our dreams coming true in the stressful reality of living will continue to give us a feeling that our lives truly are worth living.

I have to agree with Donna when she writes that the "realization that all dreams cannot and will not come true is significant to our emotional lives". However, she continues to state that "frequently, what seems failures may actually be maximum successes". Now, think about that reflective statement.

And, as I have stated earlier, I obtained every goal that I had dreamed of doing. However, even though I had reached for, and touched every goal, there still were times when those goals, eventually, developed into failures. But I still can view them as success stories because I went for what I wanted to do and my original dream became a reality.

Now, how do we define "Living The Dream"? I have heard that expression used in a very sarcastic way many times. It has been used to describe a person's situation in life in a very negative way. However, I hope to present "Living The Dream" from a positive perspective, if possible, in this presentation.

"Living The Dream", by definition in a positive way "signifies achieving everything a person has hoped for in life, typically in a career or with personal goals. It conveys a sense of satisfaction, fulfillment, and happiness in a person's current life situation, symbolizing a level of success or achievement that was previously only a dream."

As I reflect on the definition of "Living The Dream", I can honestly state that, at this stage of the journey, I feel that I have lived a very successful and rewarding life. Although I have never been, nor do I believe that I will ever be, financially successful, I have to smile when I reflect on the journey of my life. I have lived a very exciting life. People might be amazed when I tell them everything that I have done. However, personally, for me, they were just parts of my journey, See, those accomplishments do not define the true meaning of my successful and rewarding life.

For me, "Living The Dream" means that I am thankful and grateful to God for giving me a second opportunity to just be alive. When I existed in a coma for a year and a half, I was also living in a "dream world". See, what I was experiencing and doing while in the coma was real to me. And you can read about that life in my book, "THE MIRACLE OF ROOM 405". See, in a very real way, I was "living the dream". And when God returned me to this life by pushing me out of bed and smashing my face into the concrete floor of my nursing home room, I did not want to come back and leave my dreamlike life.

See, I was successful in my other "life". My wife, Sharon, was with me and my parents were alive. However, my Creator, God, had other plans for my life after showing me a brief glimpse of Eternity. Now, I understand that my Will is not always God's Will.

So, God returned me to this life for a reason. I believe that I still have work to do in this life. And there are times when I think and wonder if this life is only a dream, too. Is the life that we live in this lifetime real or really just a dream? What do you think? Maybe, we are living in a "parallel or alternate universe".

Shortly after I moved into my apartment, after recovering from my coma, an old friend from my past life telephoned me. In our conversation, I told him about the life that I had lived and my experiences while in the coma. I told him how real my life was during that time. Very interested, my friend suggested that I might have experienced life in an "alternate or parallel universe". I had never thought about that reality. However, I thought that the possibility was a fascinating perspective on my life for a year and a half.

So, what is an alternate universe or a parallel universe? Well, defined, it is "a hypothetical world that coexists with our known universe but is very different from it. It can also refer to an imaginary realm, often a variant form of the real world, depicting a different way that events could have unfolded". This definition is very real to me because that is the way I lived in my coma.

If you read my book, "THE MIRACLE OF ROOM 405", you will see and understand. See, in a very strange way, I was living my life in a dream. However, I was actually "living the dream" in a way that most people will never imagine as they live their lives in this life.

See, in the dream world" of my coma, I was doing all the things that I would be doing in this life. I was doing book signing events in Harrisburg. I was driving my 2003 Volkswagen Beetle. And I was returning to Lancaster Theological Seminary for an advanced degree. My parents were still alive and I was with my wife, Sharon, in the house that we had built. Even several of the staff members and doctors whom I knew and met after my coma were in the fantasy of my "dream world" of a coma. So, maybe, I really was "living the dream" in the fantasy world of my coma. However, I will not know if that world is true until God calls me to come and live, finally, in Eternity.

Now, as I begin to come to the end of this chapter of my journal, my life, and my legacy, I would like to reflect, briefly, on our opening quote by Shannon Adler as she presents her thoughts on leaving a legacy. "Carve your name on hearts, not on tombstones. A legacy is etched into the minds of others and the stories they share about you."

See, I have always told people to tell their friends and loved ones how they truly feel about them while both you and that person are still alive because when we die all we can talk to is a cold body in a casket or a mound of dirt at a gravesite. So, as Shannon Adler suggests, make sure part of your legacy is to "carve your name on hearts, not on tombstones" while the people you truly love and care about are still alive.

Finally, I really do believe that my legacy will be "etched" into the minds of others and the stories that they will share" by reading my books. See, the books that I have written tell the story of my life, legacy, and journey. Just like the poems and essays that I have included in this journey from my classmates from 1964 and 1965 in our high school literary arts magazine. Many of my classmates have passed from this lifetime. However, their thoughts, words, and dreams will live on in the stories that they shared in "REFLECTIONS".

See, each one of us has a unique story to tell and share about our lives. You do not need to write a book and have it published to share the journey of your life. Every person has a story within their mind and memory that will tell whoever listens to that individual about the chapters of the life of that one special individual. Now, that special individual with a unique story to tell can be the person who is reading these words. You, too, can be "LIVING THE DREAM".

Chapter 9:
"LIVING THE LEGACY"

"If your actions create a legacy that inspires others to dream more, learn more, do more, and become more, then, you are an excellent leader."

(Dolly Parton, singer-songwriter)

As we begin this chapter of my life and legacy, together, let us take a couple of brief moments to reflect on the inspirational words from Dolly Parton in our opening quote.

Later in this chapter, I will discuss the ways that we can inspire others by leaving a positive legacy for them to follow. However, for now, think about how you can leave a legacy by living your life in a positive and productive way with your actions. Here are some ways that I have tried to live my life after returning from my coma.

Inspiring your loved ones and friends is one key way to live and leave a lasting legacy. Be truthful in all your relationships. Find a career that you love and enjoy working, and support a cause that you are passionate about creating. Share your blessings with other people. Possibly, be a mentor. Follow your dreams and pursue your ambitions and passions in life. Basically, be grateful for your life, love your life and yourself, and be enthusiastic about living. I will discuss these ways and more on how to live a legacy later in this chapter.

However, the point is to show other people that your life mattered when you lived in this lifetime.

Now, allow me to return to my old high school literary arts publication, "REFLECTIONS", from 1964. I was only a junior in high school that year; however, I found an essay written by a senior that I believe reflects on the meaning and purpose of this chapter. The title of this offering is "LIFE". It was written and submitted by a student that I never knew existed until I read her words. In fact, I had to find her senior photograph in my 1964 yearbook. So, here is the reflection on "LIFE" submitted by Duane Kroneberger. I do not know if Duane is still alive; however, I do believe that the legacy of her words will live longer than her mortal lifetime in this world.

"LIFE" by Duane Kroneberger begins with a quote from Jean-Jacques Rousseau, a Swiss Enlightenment philosopher we believed that all human beings should live with two basic instincts: A sense of self-preservation and a pity for other people. "To live is not merely to breathe, it is to act."

Duane continues her reflection on Life by stating "What meaningful words these are; for life is not simply a day-to-day existence, but rather a volume of days, each of which should represent a profitable experience or progress in some degree. A vast realm of undiscovered horizons awaits our conquest - fields of science, medicine, education, literature, and the arts.

But how will these frontiers be uncovered unless every individual contributes something?

No matter how small the contribution may be, it is important that each person has the desire to want to help. Pitied should be those who have neither the interest nor the concern to lift themselves from a commonplace entity. One should not be content to rest in a state of mediocrity, inhabiting a nest of uselessness and waste, enduring his existence as if it were a casual passing of time. W. James once said 'the great use of a life is to spend it for something that outlasts it."

As I read again and reflect on the contribution submitted by Duane Kroneberger, such an insightful young girl, so long ago, in 1964, I believe that the final statement by W. James is so important, relevant, and applicable to our understanding of living and leaving a legacy for other people. "The great use of a life is to spend it for something that outlasts it." I think those words define the true meaning and purpose of living and leaving a legacy And although Jean-Jacques Rousseau and W. James are no longer alive in this world, their thoughts and words will live forever. That is their legacy.

Now, as I reflect on my life, both prior to my coma and after I returned to this life, I realize that I have wasted a lot of precious time. I have made that statement in the past in this journal; however, now, I hope that my life can be an example to you, the reader of this offering. See, my point is for you to use most of your God-given days in ways that will outlast and outlive your life here on Earth.

See, now that I have been given a new life, I realize that I have God-given talents and gifts that I need to use in the time that I have remaining in this life. Each one of us has things that we enjoy doing, things that we are good at creating, things that can give us a sense of accomplishment and a feeling of fulfillment. And when we are given time to create and accomplish our goals and use our talents, then, many other people will benefit from what we have produced. See, in that way, we are truly living our legacy when we are still alive.

As Duane Kroneberger writes in her essay, "Life is not simply a day-to-day existence, but rather a volume of days, each of which should represent a profitable experience or progress in some degree". I realize that my days are limited at this stage of my life. However, if I intend to live and leave a legacy, I do not have any more time to waste. I confess and admit that I have accumulated a "volume" of wasted days and nights in my past life in a day-to-day existence. But when I woke up from my learning experience in a coma, it did not take many days to realize that I did not want to spend, waste, or just simply exist for the remainder of my life in a nursing home. I had things to accomplish before my final "expiration due date".

See, I believe that each one of us has some contribution to give to society, no matter where we were born or what family situation we were born into. Each one of our lives was created and brought into this world for a reason and a purpose. Each one of our lives matters. We should not simply choose to just waste our lives in a useless existence and only pass the time until our lives come to an end in this lifetime.

So, how do we define "LIVING A LEGACY"? What does it mean to live a legacy while we are still alive in this life? Sadly, people live and leave legacies in both good and bad ways, in both meaningful and productive ways or in negative and destructive ways.

There are people who live and leave a legacy in both sick and healthy ways. In a sick way, think of the people who leave a legacy and are remembered for murdering an innocent human being, or sexually abusing a young child, or raping a woman. Their actions will never be forgotten or forgiven, especially with the families that suffered from their legacies.

"LIVING THE LEGACY" can simply be defined as "learning from your past, living in the present, and building for the future". As I live my life now, after returning to the reality of existing in the life of being in a coma, that straightforward way of living is how I have chosen to live the remainder of the time that God has granted me in this new life.

See, creating and living a positive and worthwhile legacy to leave other people is not something that you can achieve or accomplish after you die. It is an important part of your "Living Will", something that you hope to leave for people who will remember your life. However, I am not talking about money, assets, or property. I am focused on what you have experienced, endured, accomplished, and lived during the time you existed in this life. What really was important to you? What really was valuable in and to your life? What really do you want to be remembered for doing after your life comes to an end?

"LIVING THE LEGACY" is the way you live your life every day that you are alive. It is what you work to create and experience every day that you walk through life. It is all about letting go of your past mistakes and painful moments in time, your hurtful losses, and accepting the beautiful gift of your life every morning when you wake up to feel the wonderful breath of a new day.

"LIVING THE LEGACY" means setting new goals, aspirations, and hopes for achieving something to improve your life every day. See, you need to know your end goal. What contributions do you want to make and leave to other people? What positive impact on life do you want to be remembered for after your final "expiration date" becomes due and your "shelf life" has expired? How will your biographical obituary be written and read?

See, "LIVING A LEGACY" is all about leaving a legacy that constantly continues to be developed from a life that is dedicated to self-reflection, a life that has meaning and purpose. It is not dedicated to wasting the precious gift of life.

Leaving a legacy is and will be an important aspect of the work you have done while you lived in this life. It is a unique journal, a specific account, of what you have experienced and endured so that other people can learn from your journey in life. It is an account of what will be revealed about your life, a truthful and value-driven body of living.

Living and leaving a legacy will fulfill a need and a desire to be remembered for what you have specifically and personally contributed to society. It is all about your belief and hope that your life matters in some way.

There are several ways that a person can create, live, and leave a legacy while still living. Instead of just existing and wasting your God-given gift of life, here are a couple of ways that you can create a living legacy:

- You can pursue your passions because they can become infectious, in a positive way, to other people.

- You can choose to dedicate your life to a career field that you enjoy and love. Remember, you are only here in this life for a very limited time.

- You can be a mentor to other people who are struggling in life.

- You can set big goals in order to make the most of the limited time you have remaining in this lifetime.

- You can review the journey of your life, reflect on your life, and decide what has been the most important aspect of your journey.

- You can choose to be grateful for your life. See, when you are completely grateful for the gift of your life, then you will feel and experience a greater and deeper sense of joy.

- You can choose to be enthusiastic about life and living. The more excited you become about your life, the more you will enjoy and appreciate each new day when you open your eyes.

- You can develop a better attitude about facing the challenges of each new day. Then your positive attitude will be a reflection of the way other people will trust you.

- You can inspire other people, through your actions, to work toward accomplishing and achieving their goals.

- You can develop character and be truthful and honest in your relationships.

- You can share your blessings with other people who need help in living their lives if you have something they need.

- You can accept yourself, even with your faults, because, after all, you truly are a unique individual.

- Basically, you can show other people that you love life and love yourself for the person you have become.

Okay, now let's take a deeper look into several of the ways you can create a "Living Legacy".

As I stated, you can support causes that are important to you. For me, I am working on creating a legacy for my wife, Sharon, that will offer support, education, information, and awareness of issues pertaining to domestic violence, sexual abuse, and related eating disorders of women. Sharon died in 2005 from complications of these issues in her first marriage.

You can pursue your passionate interests. See, your passions can become your legacy. A passion is developed from an outpouring of the interests, thoughts, and ideas that make up a significant difference in our lives. Finding, seeing, and pursuing your passions will allow you to envision your destiny in a more focused and clearer way. And, to pursue your passions and interests to the fullest can be contagious to other people. So, always try to think of new adventures to follow in your life.

You can choose to dedicate your life to a career field that you truly enjoy. So, find the type of work that really and truly invigorates you. Find a cause that you are deeply passionate about because that cause will help you to create your "Living Legacy".

You can become a mentor to other people who respect you. I believe that everyone has some significant truth to show and share with others that will guide less experienced people in life.

You can reflect on and choose what are the most important aspects of your life and write about them. Review the journey of your life. How did you transform your life? How did you make the necessary changes in your life when you had to take a different direction? Did you inspire other people to change their lives? Did you ever touch the lives of other people? Did you live a joyful and purpose-filled life?

You can choose to be grateful for the gift of your life. What is your attitude about life and living? How did you develop positive coping skills? Are you looking for the brighter side of life or only choosing to exist in the dark? See, your attitude about life and living will always be a reflection of other people who look at you and the way they see and trust you. And, when you are completely joyful and grateful about your life, then it will not matter how much outer success you have because you will never enjoy your accomplishments and achievements. So, take the time to appreciate the small moments of happiness that have been given to you.

You can choose to be enthusiastic about your life because the more you project enjoyment about living and appreciate each and every day when you open your eyes to a new beginning, it will be reflected in the lives of people who come into your life that day who might be living under a cloud.

You can accept the uniqueness of yourself. You can be completely comfortable in accepting yourself as a person and that acceptance will be reflected in the lives of those people who you interact with on a daily basis. See, no one else can write the book that you were destined to write. Always know and remember that you were born with amazing strengths to challenge and overcome any obstacle in your walk through life.

Finally, the goal of "LIVING THE LEGACY" is to love yourself. Always love the life that God has granted and given to you. Always cherish each new day and always appreciate the limited amount of time that you have been granted in this lifetime by your Creator.

Chapter 10:
"MY LEGACY"

"WE ALL DIE. The goal is not to live forever, but to leave behind something that will."

(Chuck Palahniuk, author)

There are only a couple of things that are certain in life and living. One of them is found in the first line of our opening quote by Chuck Palahnuik. "WE ALL DIE." Truer words were never written or spoken. The reality of each one of our lives is that it will come to an end, eventually. For many of us, in an unexpected way. So, as we begin this chapter, please take a couple of minutes to reflect on our opening quote. My question to you is what will you leave behind that people will remember about your life? What will be your legacy?

A couple of days ago, very unexpectedly, I received a "friend" request from someone whom I had not heard from in fourteen years. It was a request from my goddaughter, Julie. I had not seen or heard from Julie since I officiated her wedding and performed her marriage ceremony in May of 2010. Of course, I accepted her request. I knew that she had something very important to tell me. Although, I was very surprised that Julie had found me after all these years. I wondered how she had located me.

Painfully, Julie informed me that her father had died. That news was a surprising shock for me. Jimmy was my second partner in narcotics when we were both police detectives during the 1970s. I really did not want another partner after my blood brother, P. J., died. I did not want to get close to anyone else. However, Jimmy and I had something in common. We were both ex-Baltimore City Police officers. Although, Jimmy chose not to go on strike and I did. We were both in the police academy at about the same time. I was one class before him.

Although I had a difficult time developing trust with Jimmy, we became very good friends. After all, if you cannot trust your partner, then who can you trust, especially working undercover?

I had not seen or heard from Jimmy since Julie's wedding in 2010. However, I never forgot about him because we had created a bond that would last as long as the two of us were alive. But Jimmy moved to Texas and we lost contact with each other. Julie informed me that her father had died from complications related to chronic lymphocytic leukemia and Parkinson's Disease originating from exposure to Agent Orange when he was in Vietnam during the war. Sadly, I thought about the times Jimmy and I worked undercover in narcotics for the next two days and I was reminded and reminisced about all the dangerous things we did that could have ended our lives during that time.

I still have pictures of us placed on my living room wall reflecting the way we looked undercover during the 1970s. Those pictures are Jimmy's legacy to me and I will cherish them until the day I die. Then, I came to the realization that Jimmy and I were the same age. I began to think about the end of my life and wondered when that day would come for me.

Then, I began to think about some unanswered questions in my life.

- How will I be remembered?

- How do I want to be remembered?

- What have I really accomplished in my life?

- What lessons did I learn along the way?

- What do I want to leave behind when I die?

- Does anyone really know the "real me"?

As I stated earlier in this journal, everyone will leave a legacy, whether or not they plan or intend to leave one. See, everything we say or do in life will leave an imprint, a footprint, of our journey in this life.

So, what really is a legacy? Well, a legacy can be defined in several ways. However, for me, since I am not financially wealthy and never will be rich, I believe that I am still leaving a rich legacy in several other ways.

See, for me, a legacy can be defined as the long-lasting impact of my life on my friends, family, those who knew me, and those people who knew of me.

However, this journal of my journey in life is primarily based on a "Theological Perspective of the Meaning of Life", as discussed in Chapter Three of this book. So, let us begin by reflecting on what the holy Christian Bible says about a legacy.

The Bible tells us that a good legacy is one that teaches a good inheritance by being gracious with our time and energy, not only with our money. It tells us that we should place our trust in God to supply us with everything that we need according to the Will of God. Basically, the holy Christian Bible teaches us that a good legacy to leave is based on living uprightly and faithfully before God and other people. Now, I have to confess that I did not always live my life in that way before God put me in a coma. I realize and understand why God put me in a coma for basically a short period of time. I realize that the year and a half that I existed in the coma was not a waste of time. Actually, I was given an extension on my life in the hope of learning a valuable lesson before my final "expiration date" finally will come due.

In the Holy Christian Bible, a legacy is defined as "a lasting spiritual and moral impact that you can leave for future generations. It involves living a life in alignment with God's Word and Will, influencing others for Jesus Christ".

See, a biblical legacy is all about the "standing stones" that you place throughout your life as you work to pass values, lessons of faith, and "inner wealth" on to future generations.

It is not about the headstones that are placed on your grave after you die. Then, it will be too late to leave a legacy. Then people will only be looking at a pile of dirt.

You need to remember that a legacy involves living intentionally and always aiming to build on the next generations for their success. That gift is what I was given by my God in my resurrection from the coma.

In Psalm 145:4 of the Holy Christian Bible, we read "One generation shall praise your works to another and shall declare Your mighty Acts". Of course, this scripture is referring to the work of God. However, my hope is that I will be remembered by the people in and through the good things that I have done and accomplished in the short time that I have lived in this life.

Now, what will be "MY LEGACY"? Earlier, I have listed several ways that a person can leave a legacy. However, my priority for the remainder of my life is to focus on creating a legacy for my wife, Sharon. You can read about Sharon in my book about her life in "SHARON'S LIGHT". She changed my life in a way that she never realized while she was alive. So, maybe how Sharon made me stronger is really her legacy to me.

However, my hope for other people is to show anyone that he or she can accomplish almost any goal if you set your mind on achieving it. In the pages of my books, you can see that I set big goals for myself in the life I lived prior to my coma. Whatever, I wanted to work on, I went for it, even when the outcome was not successful.

In my life, I have been:

- A trumpet player in the high school marching and concert band,

- A drummer in a rock band,

- A Graphic Arts Illustrator in the Air Force with assignments in Southeast Asia, Taiwan, and Vietnam,

- A Printed Circuit Draftsman,

- A Graphic Arts Illustrator for the Bureau of Customs in Washington, D. C.,

- An insurance agent for the Prudential Insurance Company,

- A police officer,

- An undercover police detective living and working in drug groups and organized crime associations. However, I do have to state that when I resigned from the police department, I had three contracts to kill me out on my life. Two attempts were almost successful,

- A licensed private detective. I created my own private detective agency,

- An Ordained Minister serving in parish ministry after graduating from a three-year seminary,

- A drug and alcohol treatment counselor,

- A private counselor and therapist after creating my own counseling agency,

- A magazine publisher. I created and published two magazines,

- A chaplain for a strip club,

- A published author. I have written five books on the founding Gurus of the Sikh Faith. I have also written and published five other books about my life.

Along with all those creative professional ventures and adventures, I also graduated with three university degrees.

I have to confess that there have been many moments in my life since I have returned to this life from existing in a coma when I have thought about how blessed I have been in the time that I have lived. I believe those times should be a big part of the legacy that I will leave to people in the hope that they, too, can appreciate their lives.

As I have written, as a child, I was very shy and timid. I had very little self-esteem or confidence in myself. Then, in my senior year of high school, I became an alcoholic. From 1965 to 1989, my addiction to alcohol controlled my life. Although I achieved many goals during those years, I also failed many times. However, I never quit moving forward with God's guidance and direction.

I will always believe and be very thankful to God for finally directing me into a seminary. I believe the primary reason that I went to seminary was to save my life, although, I received ordination in the process.

See, I had thoughts of suicide in my mind for several years because of my life undercover as a police detective in narcotics and organized crime. However, I believe that God directed my life into seminary to save my life in treatment for my addiction and let go of those suicidal ideations.

I could not graduate from seminary and receive ordination unless I accepted treatment for my alcoholism. I have not had a drink of alcohol since February 21, 1989. Ironically, I entered treatment to begin a new life on my birthday, February 21st.

Hopefully, part of my legacy will be in the form of inspiration. I hope that the story of my life and how I overcame life-threatening challenges will inspire others to take a leap of faith in their lives.

I believe that the major focus of my legacy should not be about self-efficacy or boasting about what I have done or accomplished in my life. My hope is the words that I write will, in some way, motivate other people and give them a stronger form of confidence to pursue, accomplish, and achieve their personal goals in life.

I hope the story of my life will motivate people to pursue their individual positive passions in life, even if they have doubts in their abilities, at times. All they need is faith in God and faith in themselves.

As I continue to reflect on my life toward the end of this journal, I feel the need to be honest with people in the limited time that I have remaining in this lifetime. See, for many years, I have told people, in therapy when I was a therapist, that no one really knows what the other person is really thinking in their minds, even in close relationships like marriage.

So, as part of my legacy, I want to confess that, many times, my outward, often very sarcastic sense of humor hid my true inner insecurities. All my life, since the early years of my childhood, I rarely have been confident in any of my professional ventures or relationships, including marriage. That is the primary reason why my first marriage failed.

However, now that God has given me a second opportunity to live, I realize that we only have a very limited time to live and no one really knows when that time will come to an end and our biological clock will stop ticking. For that reason, part of my legacy is to share my weaknesses and limitations in the hope that people will learn from my lessons in life.

The legacy of my lessons can be found in the five books that I have written. They tell my story. See, now I realize why

I have written those books. I do not have any family to remember my legacy.

Another very important part of my legacy is to share my belief and faith in God. See, I have always believed in God; however, it was not until I returned to this life from the coma that my faith in God and my belief in myself became stronger. I believe God put me in a coma so I could find my way to Eternity one day in the future.

When I was told by the physical and occupational therapists in the nursing and rehabilitation center that I would never walk again, at least not without support, I would not accept their belief and diagnosis. I realized that I had to believe in God and believe in myself if I was to ever walk away from the safety and security of that nursing home.

When I was told that if I was ever able to leave the nursing home, then I would be better off living in an assisted living facility because I would not be able to take care of myself. Again, I refused to accept those conditions. I knew God would direct me if I had the courage to believe in my abilities.

When I was told that I was required to have a surgeon sign off and approve me in order to drive again, I refused to accept that condition. I renewed my driver's license and got my car out of storage. Now, I know God is riding with me and I believe in myself to get me where I need to go in life.

So, my legacy includes sharing what I have been taught and what I have learned in life, especially after returning to this life from the death of existing in a coma.

I have learned to be grateful and appreciate the unique gift of my life. Now, I cherish each new day that I can open my eyes, not only on bright, sunny days, but, also, when the weather is dark and stormy in the forecast. See, even on dark days, I believe that the sun will, eventually, rise and shine again.

In the end, I hope my legacy will show and tell people that I was very enthusiastic about life and living, that I accepted myself for the unique person that I am, even with all my faults, and that I loved the person I became in life. See, for me, life mattered.

As I close this chapter of my life, I leave you with these thoughts. As you look back over your life, remember that it is not too difficult to believe that what you experienced, went through, and lived through was all for a purpose. Everything in your life may well have been planned by God to make you of some use to other people in this world.

See, each person's life is like the pattern of a mosaic. Each thing that happened to you is like one tiny stone in the mosaic, and each tiny stone will fit into the perfected pattern of the larger mosaic of your life, which has been designed by God. You might not see the whole design of your life today.

However, all you need to do is trust and believe in the Great Designer.

"The choices we make about the lives we live determine the kinds of legacies we live and leave." (Tavis Smily)

Chapter 11:
"BACK TO THE FUTURE"

"What you leave behind is not what is engraved in stone monuments, but what is woven into the lives of others."

(Pericles, philosopher)

As I begin to reflect on this final chapter of my journal, I need to, first, think about our opening quote from Pericles. See, it really does not matter to me if anything is engraved on my tombstone. My intention is to be cremated and have my ashes blended together with the ashes of my wife, Sharon. However, I have been thinking deeply about how and what people will remember about me. I doubt if my life will be remembered long after I die of this life. I wonder if you have ever really thought about how you will be remembered.

For me, I think about my life as an "unfinished symphony". Think about that description. What really is a symphony? Briefly defined, a symphony is "an elaborate musical composition that is, typically, created in four movements". See, in a strange way, that is how I think about my life now. Four movements or in four distinct parts: Birth, Life, Death, and Rebirth.

And the "symphony" of my life is still "unfinished" because I have been "Reborn" in order to complete some unfinished work and goals that I have not been shown and made visible, yet, in my life. See, I believe that I am living in the fourth and last movement of my "symphony" in this life, the "FINALE".

I had to smile when I thought about the title of this final chapter, "BACK TO THE FUTURE". Because, in a way, it describes the journey of my life at this stage of existence. Originally, "BACK TO THE FUTURE" was a Sci-Fi comedy movie produced in 1985. It is a classic. The movie starred Michael J. Fox and Christopher Lloyd. Ironically, Michael J. Fox has been suffering and living with severely debilitating Parkinson's Disease for many years. I have also been diagnosed with Parkinson's Disease. However, fortunately for me, my condition, although there is no known cure, is not seriously restricting my activities or my life. I can still function and create.

Well, in the movie, Marty McFly (Michael J. Fox) is sent back in time by his friend, Professor Doctor Emmett Brown (Christopher Lloyd). Marty meets the two people who will, eventually, marry and become his parents. His task is to see that they really do fall in love and get married so Marty can be born and come into this world, into this life.

See, as I believe I can relate to "BACK TO THE FUTURE", the movie, I think my Creator, God, placed me in a brief coma so I could go back in time and envision my future in Eternity. Why was I only in a coma for a brief period of time and then brought back to this life?

I was informed in the nursing and rehabilitation center that the surgeon who saved my life when he drained the two liters of fluid from my brain that he had, originally, intended to put a shunt inside me. However, he stopped when he realized that if he did the surgery to install the shunt, he would kill me. See, God saved my life, again.

I, now, believe that I had to go back in time and live part of my life again so that I could see into the future. I was living in a past lifetime with my parents, my favorite aunt, and my wife, Sharon. They were all alive. I was, also, returning to seminary, again. I was doing book signings, again. Now, I believe that life will be that way when I live in Eternity with my mother, my father, my favorite Aunt Mary, and my wife, Sharon. After all, that is what I pray for every morning and every night.

As I continue with the introduction to this final chapter of the last book that I will ever write, I return to the beginning of this journal of my journey.

See, I began my Introduction to this journey by describing the walk that I was taking on a dark, grey, overcast, and surreal Christmas Eve in the final week of 2023. Now, I think it is very ironic that I am finishing this journal of my journal almost four months later, in April of 2024, following the celebration of Easter.

For me, as a Christian, and an ordained minister, that connection is very significant and symbolic. And if you are also of the Christian Faith and Belief, you will understand my thoughts.

See, in our Christian Faith and Belief, Christmas is the time when we celebrate the birth of our Savior, Jesus Christ. We celebrate this event in the dead of Winter, during the darkest time of the year when the days are the shortest in times of sunlight. Jesus Christ was born in the darkest of times.

Then, in our Christian Faith, we celebrate the death of Jesus and His Resurrection, then, after three days of death, Jesus returns to life and living as He fulfills the prophecy of the Old Testament of the Holy Christian Bible. For me, this moment in history has personal implications as it pertains to the resurrection of my life, my new life, and my renewed faith in God.

Think of the title that I chose for this book, "A TIME TO BE BORN, A TIME TO LIVE, AND A TIME TO DIE". I, now, believe that this is my time as I prepare, daily, for the coming of my mortal death.

As I have written earlier in this chapter, I began this journal on Christmas Eve, during the darkest and coldest days of Winter. For me, "Winter" is the fourth and final stage of life and living. It is like the fourth movement of an "unfinished" symphony. It is the "Finale". However, we need to remember that "darkness" is only a temporary condition. See, eventually, the sun will rise again and we will be able to feel the warmth of a new morning, a new day, a new life.

As I reflect on my Christian beliefs, I think that we celebrate the birth of our Savior, Jesus Christ, in the dead of dark Winter months as being very symbolic. Again, "darkness" is only temporary. And, I, now, can see the symbolism of the ending of this journal, the completion of this book, coming in April as Christians have recently celebrated the death and resurrection of Jesus Christ.

See, after Jesus died on the cross, He was resurrected in three days and then He was lifted up into Heaven, into Eternity, to be with His Father. In a strange way, I believe that God returned me to this life so I can finish and complete my work and then I will return to Eternity to remain with my parents, my Aunt Mary, and my wife, Sharon. For me. The warm feeling of Springtime is compared to a feeling of "rebirth" and renewal following the dark death of Winter.

Now, as I continue to write this final chapter of this journal, I go "BACK TO THE FUTURE" as I walk around my small apartment and look, once again, at everything that I listed in my Introduction. What I find most significant and important in my life at this stage of the journey is the picture that I have placed above my bed. As I explained in the Introduction, this picture was given to me on the night of my ordination into the ministry by my home church congregation, Trinity United Church of Christ, in 1989. The picture simply projects the hands of Jesus Christ reaching out as He sits. You can only see His hands and the robe He is wearing. I have placed this picture directly over the center of my bed.

In my mind, I believe that Jesus is reaching out to protect me in the darkness of the night as I sleep. I cannot go to sleep until I say my prayers and look up to those hands that are reaching out to hold me. Then, I can feel safe as I repeat the old prayer that my mother taught me when I was a very little boy. "If I should die before I wake. I pray to the Lord, my soul to take." See, that prayer is part of my mother's legacy to me.

Every night, as I look around my dark bedroom before I try to fall asleep, I feel safe and at peace. I look at the pictures on the walls. The pictures are of my parents, my favorite Aunt Mary, my wife, Sharon, and the hands of Jesus reaching out to protect me. Then I realize that I am not alone. They are all still with me in spirit. I know that I am never really alone in this life.

As I reflect on the legacy that my parents gave to me, I go back to the future, again, in the Introduction of this journal. I feel the touch of my mother and father when I hold the picture frame with the bronze baby shoes and look at my baby picture. See, the legacy that my parents gave to me was unconditional love. No matter how much trouble I got into in my life, my mother and father always loved me. However, I never realized or appreciated their love until after they had passed from this life.

Upon reflection, as I work toward the completion of this journal, I have realized that a significant contribution to my story was discovered in the two old high school publications that were saved by people I did not know before I moved into my apartment to begin my new life.

Throughout this journal of the journey of my life, I have included several poems and essays from classmates, friends, and students that were published in "REFLECTIONS", our high school literary arts magazine from Brooklyn Park High School in Anne Arundel County, Maryland. Although our high school has been closed for many years, and in a strange way, the building of brick and mortar has died, the memories and the school spirit remain and live on.

See, although I had kept those two publications of "REFLECTIONS" from 19964 and 1965, I never really read the contents of the contributions. I never knew or appreciated the insights of so many talented young students, several of whom are no longer living, until I began to feel their spirits as I researched this book. So, in a very significant, powerful, and unexpected way, the two people who saved these publications for me have played an indescribable and extremely unusual part in taking me "BACK TO THE FUTURE".

As I begin to walk toward the end of this journey, I reflect on the interesting and very ironic walk that I took on Easter Sunday of this year. If you can remember, I began this journal on Christmas Eve, 2023. I have described the weather conditions on that day.

Now, also, remember that my story is coming to an end in April, four months later, near the celebration of Easter, signifying the resurrection and rising of Jesus Christ, three days after his crucifixion and death on a cross.

Well, on this Easter Sunday, I began my walk around Lewisburg, just as I had done many times before since I moved to this location. However, this time became very ironic and after I finished my journey, I had to smile.

See, when I began my walk, the weather conditions were similar to those of my walk on Christmas Eve, four months earlier. However, this was to be Springtime. But it did not feel like Spring. The temperature was cold for this time of the year. The sky was dark, grey, and overcast, similar to the conditions on Christmas Eve.

When I began my walk, I thought about turning back because it was so cold and windy. However, I had not walked for a couple of weeks, so I decided to continue on my journey. In total, I physically walked for an hour. However, I needed to stop for a rest about halfway.

On my walking routine, when I stop for a rest, I always look up to the sky, smile, and talk to my mother, my father, my Aunt Mary, and my wife, Sharon. Then, I thank God for the gift of my ability to walk following my stroke. This time, after I talked to everyone and thanked God for this day, I began to walk, again. Ironically, at this moment, the sun began to shine and the temperature began to get warmer. I could feel the change in the weather and I had to smile.

See, for me, this was a very symbolic sign. It was Easter Sunday and I realized the significance of the change in the weather with my belief in the Risen Christ. In my mind, Jesus Christ had truly risen from the darkness of death and now the sunshine of new life was shining and reflecting a bright light for me. The darkness of Winter was gone. Once again, I was walking in the Springtime of my life. I felt a stronger sense of energy as I walked back to my apartment complex. I truly did feel that I had walked "BACK TO THE FUTURE".

When I returned to my apartment, I, immediately, walked into my bedroom and looked at the large Crucifix that I had placed on the wall near my bed. See, I realized that the significance of the cross and what it represented was also part of my legacy. I wear the cross, with Jesus Christ hanging on it, around my neck and I am never alone or without it.

On the desk, under the cross on the wall, I still have my original Rosary. It was given to me when I was a very little boy. I received the Rosary, along with a prayer book, when I made my First Holy Communion at Saint Rose of Lima Roman Catholic Church in Baltimore, Maryland. I still have the prayer book.

My Rosary is ironically unique. When I was living undercover as a police detective in drug groups and organized crime associations, I always carried my Rosary as a combination of good luck and protection. Well, one night, I accidentally sat on the Rosary and broke off the left arm of

Jesus. From that moment, He was only hanging on the cross with His right hand. However, I always cherished that old Rosary. It was part of my childhood.

Ironically, after I returned to this life from the living death of my coma, a couple of items were returned to me very quickly. One of them was my old Rosary. However, now, Jesus Christ was completely missing from the Cross. I still have no understanding why He was removed. However, in my mind, I truly believe that Jesus was taken from the Crucifix on my Rosary as a sign. I truly believe that Jesus Christ is missing from the Crucifix of my Rosary as a sign that He truly was Resurrected. See, for me, it is a sign that I was also resurrected from the death of my coma and returned to this life. That belief is also part of my legacy.

Now, as I come to the end of this journal, the "FINALE" of my "unfinished symphony" of my life, I still have so many unanswered questions. Although I know the reason that I began to write this story, I still wonder what part of my life, if any, will live long after my mortal life ceases to exist in this lifetime. Will it be as if my life never existed? Will I be forgotten? Will the memory of my life disappear forever?

As I look in the mirror at night before I lay down for rest, I realize that I live alone. However, deep within my being, I know and believe that I am never really alone when I close my eyes and try to fall asleep. In my heart and mind, I know that God is with me in the darkness of the night.

Maybe, someone will add these words to my eulogy or inscribe them on my death certificate and memorial when I am cremated:

"In my life,
I have lived,
I have loved,
I have lost,
I have won,
I have hurt,
I have been hurt,
I have trusted,
I have lost trust,
I have made mistakes,
However,
Above all,
I have learned."

Now, here is my prayer for you, the reader, as we come to the end of our journey, together.

"Miracles happen every day in the lives of people.
Always know and believe that there is a power available to help you do the right thing in life.
My hope is that you accept that power.
The miracles that will happen in your life will be evidence of God's Power.
I pray that you do not need to see the whole design of your life.

I pray that you only need to trust the Designer.
I pray that you may take each day as a gift from God.
I pray that you may thank God for each new day and be grateful in it.
I pray that you will not come empty to the end of your life.
I pray that you may live so that you will not be afraid to die."

Finally, because this contribution is focused on leaving a legacy, in the end, I would like to submit several contributions from my high school friends and classmates. The following poems will live as legacies from individuals who had dreams and visions at such a young age. I hope that some of these once young lives are still living. Their legacies are recorded in the pages of our literary arts magazine published by the students of Brooklyn Park High School, once located on Hammonds Lane, in Anne Arundel County, Maryland. The publications are from 1964 and 1965. Their contributions, along with so many other submissions, have inspired me to write this book.

From Charles Blevins: ADVICE TO AN IDLE MIND

"Idle Mind,
Cease squandering Thyself in senseless thought.
Come, master the meaning of life,
Rejoice in the sweetness of youth,
Explore Memory's deep caverns,
Look upon love and beauty.
Laggard One,
Waste not a precious moment,
But live, that thy record of existence
Be etched in labor and laughter."

From Joseph Hartman: THOUGHTS ON DEATH

"A moist cloud enshrouds my being,
Smothering all life
Until I am nothing.
 My steps led to that point
 From whence there is no returning.
Sweet life was taken
But all doubts are gone."

From Bette Hancock: SING, OH SING!

"Sing, sweet Bird of Happiness,
To all the world impart.
 The purport of your existence
In every human heart!
 Many there are about you
Who cherish and bless the time,

You use to bestow your glorious gift
Of laughter and pleasure sublime.
 When your task is finished
And your message complete,
 Send us us your brother, Love,
To relay his purposes deep.
 Send him o'er the oceans
And through the walls of sin,
 That he may nurture peace and joy
That mankind holds within.
 Bring him to the bedside
Of those lost in despair;
 Have him voice the way of Hope
That all who hear may share.
 Oh, sing, sweet Bird of Goodness,
Sing to brighten Lifed's highway
That its hardships we may withstand.
 Sing until you are breathless;
Let your melodies ring!
 Banish all grief and sorrow;
Sing, Bird of Happiness, sing!"

From Walter Balint: PARADISE OF A SAILOR

"The sea is quiet now.
 Gone is the wind and rain and hail.
 The time has come when the sailor may
 Look upon God's world and say:
 'I love the sky, the sea, the foam,

May this be my eternal home.'

When the night fails, deep silence prevails,
As God's hands press against the sails.
And now the sailor can understand
Why all the people who dwell on land
Feel not so close to God as he
While sailing across his star-lit sea.

Someday his life will come to end;
His soul to heaven, God will send.
While his body will be consigned to the deep
Where no man may ever disturb his sleep.
The sailor loves his life at sea,
And there his holy grave will be."

From Madeline Synowski: ETERNAL SEESAW

"Life is a tiny ship, timid and uncertain,
    Tossed about by an angry sea.
Its rain-drenched masts are the joys and sorrows of all
mankind.
    And we are its grasping crew.

At intervals, the stormy waters rise and envelop one of the
crew
    In its cloak of darkness.
    Bird our cunning vessel barters
With its artless foe, and receives, for every bereavement,
    A new name on the roster of her crew.
    She resumes her course,

125

And upon her mast, a new sail is placed.
Strong and steady, ready for another storm,
It stands there, waiting,
Symbolizing Nature's perfect balance.

Bonus Chapter: "FRIENDS BEFORE YOU"

Life can be incredibly interesting and very unpredictable at times. Case in point, my many years of very close friendship with the contributor of this essay. I have been fortunate to know and cherish Carlyl Pike for more years than I can remember. I cannot recall the exact year that she came into my life. I cannot remember why she came into my life. All I can say is that Carlyl came into my life in a past life. No, I am not thinking about a form of reincarnation. However, I am talking about my life before I went into a coma.

Now, "Carlyl Pike" is not her real name. It is the pen name she has chosen to work with in her writing. Really, who would name their child "Carlyl Pike"? It sounds like a major highway near Mechanicsburg, Pennsylvania, the Carlisle Pike. Although, my forever friend is originally from Pennsylvania.

Maybe, she would not want to admit it; however, Carlyl Pike is a very creative and talented woman. She is working on and writing two books. She has recorded a song. And, she has contributed several short stories that are in another one of my books, "DARK SOUL"

I have only physically seen "Carlyl" one time. Although, she has proven to me that we have met on two occasions. See, our first physical meeting took place when she drove a long distance when I was in a coma. I was so disappointed when she showed me pictures of her visit and I did not know that she was near me.

Actually, we met on Facebook many years ago. I cannot remember what attracted me to her or why I requested her friendship on Facebook. However, I really do believe in destiny. I believe that Carlyl Pike and I were destined to meet in this life for some reason.

Since that initial unexpected connection so many years ago, we have developed a special bond that will last a lifetime.

Now, I present to you a wonderful and beautiful essay written by an incredible and gifted individual to end this journal. Please enjoy 'FRIENDS BEFORE YOU".

"FRIENDS BEFORE YOU"

I call it, 'FRIENDS BEFORE YOU". Stop and just think about that statement for a moment. It does not mean what you think it means, it is deeper. Think deep into your heart. Friends who are born prior to you, which means they are older, born before you. The best kind of friends have been there, they understand, and they say "Been there, done that".

For the most part, optimistic, and confident, live in the moment, friends. You will find them less dramatic, altruistic, genuine, grateful, empathetic, witty, positive, unapologetic, and unfiltered, which is just a slight taste of their golden qualities.

My grandmother passed away when I was only nine. I hardly knew her. She left us far too early in life. She spoke Italian and as a young child, growing up in the 60s, I did not speak her language. However, I did understand her way of communicating with me in a childlike fashion. She would reach into the pockets of her dress and pull out somewhat melted Hershey kisses in the palm of her hand to give to me. Her playful way of reaching out to her grandchildren to show how much she loved us. I only wish I could have spoken to her and asked her as many questions, as I could to learn about her.

My parents met each other and began to start their family in their late 20s and 30s, understandably older, wiser, strict, and somewhat exhausted. They would participate in our school and our extracurricular activities, as much as they possibly could, trying not to spread themselves too thin with the four of us, without exhaustion. I was always surrounded by older people, all my relatives, aunts, uncles, and most of my cousins who were mostly older than me. Even the neighborhood children, I tended to gravitate toward the older children in our neighborhood to hang out with and have fun. I never thought about the age difference at the time because there was always someone there to spend time with or look out for me and have my back. They were so ahead of the game that I learned a lot from them. My father worked full-time and my mother stayed home full-time to take care of us. My father worked from 3 o'clock in the afternoon until 11 o'clock at night, which allowed my mother to be the one who had the most quality time with all of us. My mother would attend most of our PTA meetings. How well I remember those reports of the parent-teacher meetings when she would return home. I was guaranteed a lecture from my mother on how I was very talkative in my classes and needed to pay more attention in school.

As a child growing up, I did what almost all children were expected to do. My parents enrolled me in kindergarten, elementary school, middle school, and then high school. I attended an out-of-state college in Maryland. I studied arts and science and also got a degree in dental hygiene. During my college years, I made friends, and most of these friends, again, were older than me. My neighbors in the building had all graduated and were working in the city. Some of them would help me with projects and reports after school. Some of my professors became friends of mine during college and after graduating. They were like second parents to me. I always cherished the relationships that I have made with them.

I moved to South Carolina and began to seek employment as a dental hygienist. I found a nice working environment in an office that became my second home. Of course, I made friends with the people I worked with, and most of all, with some of the patients that came for our dental services. They were encouraging and a lovely group of good, genuine Southern, mild-mannered people that welcomed this Yankee, with open arms.

After several years, I left South Carolina and moved to Florida. Upon moving to Florida, where three-fourths of the population is over 65. I decided to work out of several different offices as a part-time, permanent, or fill-in dental hygienist. The rotation of the clientele could be quite challenging. I have always enjoyed most of the patients who came in and out of the practices during the course of my dental career.

Some patients I found to be wonderful, weathered, whiny, witty, wild, welcoming, willing, very wealthy, and wanderlust. (For fun, I wanted to use words that start with "W"). For the most part, I have found many patients to be intriguing, most in particular were actually the "friends before me" patients. Meaning the "mature seasoned" patients. For fun, those patients who love to speak about their life experiences, their past careers, what they found to be their biggest accomplishments, the relationships with their spouses/partners, how long they were married, their families, ie: (their children, grandchildren, parents, and grandparents). I would enjoy asking about the most humorous moments and most interesting moments of their lives, what countries they loved to travel to, and why, if they had any regrets, and which automobiles they found that were more fascinating than others. The male patients would give you a full consumer report in the chair, boasting of their past and present expensive automobiles. It was great fun, learning about these patients, and picking their minds, getting to know a bit about them, their likes and dislikes. I believe they enjoyed engaging in such conversation. Oftentimes, they would say "thank you" and say "Other clinicians were not so interested in getting to know about them" like I did. Some shared with me just about anything and everything. Maybe, just a bit too much information at times, where it became a little bit weird in their next return visit, knowing what I knew from them.

Some have shared what experiences they found fascinating and what they felt was overrated. Interestingly enough, I giggled when one "seasoner" said to me that she thought children were overrated, or at least, she felt all of hers were, and reminded me of how lucky I was that I had not reproduced, and to count my blessings!! Loved her, and her bold statement.

There was one special lady in particular who came into the office for a cleaning, every other month, her teeth were so heavily stained from smoking a pipe. Yes, I said a pipe. She mentioned to me that she and her husband shared that habit together after dinner every evening for as long as they were married. He passed away prior to her, while she continued this terrible habit until her death at the age of 91. I met her ten years before her death, which means that she had been smoking a pipe for almost her entire "seasoned" life. I was always so excited to see her name on the schedule and to know that she was still alive and keeping up with her bad habit. Together, we had such fun catching up during her dental visit/dental lecture. She never filtered her language around me, or anyone else for that fact. She said what she wanted to say, and how she wanted to say it, unapologetically. I loved that about her.

So, I will admit that MOST all of these "seasoned" patients or "friends before me" patients or "friends waaaay before me" patients; however, you wish to categorize these special and beautiful people, most certainly brightened my day, lifted my spirits, and educated me on future behavior that I may indulge in as life goes forward for me. An authentic group of honest energy, well beyond their golden years, that is full of verbal surprises, and leaves you with laughter and touches your soul as friends do…

Over the course of my life, by having friends that were/are older, some, much older, I can relate to people older than me for whatever reason, perhaps from my surroundings as a youth. I feel that I can continue to learn from them and have their bravery. Perhaps, because I feel that they feel they are closer to death and that is where they have genuine appreciation for those who take an interest in them. I am sure we think about death more often as we age. Honestly, I know I do, and there is nothing that any of us can do to make ourselves not think that way, it is natural. However, there is an abundance of what we can do to make ourselves think young again, act young again, live life as young again as we can, and try to continue to have the mindset of our youth, yet again. By having "seasoned" friends helps to relate to what they may be thinking and what they may be facing themselves about their past and present experiences of their life's journey.

One day, we will be in their place. They will step out, leave us, and we will be the next ones to move into their spot. We will cherish what we have learned from them because we have taken the time to talk with them and inherit their bravery.

As the old saying goes, the golden principle of testing others, as one would expect to be treated themselves. Let us learn from one another, never turn your back on a friend. We all need to be patient and kind to those "seasoned" people and to "all people".

As for me, I was honored to have serviced these fine individuals. Each one has left a lasting impact, some of my most valued experiences in life. I hope that I can continue to have the insight to learn about people and to dig deeper into other fine souls, as I have. I will always cherish the friendships that I have made. They all have left me with a rich legacy of knowledge. May this continue for others.

LIFE IS A BLESSING,
Carlyl Pike

Dedicated to Michelle and Tyler.
There is no race in life, do not be in any hurry.
Make time for others, especially for "seasoned friends".
Thank you for bringing so much love into our family.

With love,
Your Auntie

135